4.1.1 GLOBALISATION

What you need to know

Characteristics of globalisation

Factors contributing to globalisation in the last 50 years

Impacts of globalisation and global companies on individual countries, governments, producers and consumers, workers and the environment

What is globalisation?

Globalisation is a process by which economies and cultures have been drawn deeper together and have become more interconnected through global networks of trade, capital flows, and the rapid spread of technology and global media. The share of global GDP accounted for by exports of goods and services has risen from 12% in 1960 to almost 30% now.

What is the key benefit of globalisation?

Globalisation allows businesses and countries to specialise in producing goods and services where they have a comparative advantage (i.e. able to produce at a lower opportunity cost – this topic is covered in more detail later in this study book). Specialisation and trade enable a gain in economic welfare, for example through lower prices for consumers which then increases their real incomes. It also allows consumers to buy a greater range of goods/services, increasing choice.

Quick question
Think back to goods/services you have consumed this week – which might have had some element of their production carried out abroad?

Characteristics of globalisation

- Trade to GDP ratios are increasing for many countries
- Expansion of financial capital flows across international borders 
- Increasing foreign direct investment and cross border acquisitions 
- More global brands – including a rising number from emerging countries 
- Deeper specialisation of labour e.g. in making specific component parts 
- Global supply chains and new trade and investment 
- Higher levels of crossborder labour migration 
- Increasing connectivity of people and businesses through networks 

Factors contributing to globalisation in the last 50 years

1. **Containerisation** – the real prices and costs of ocean and air shipping have come down due to the widespread use of standardised containers and reaping of economies of scale in freight industries and often huge container ports built to serve them. This reduces the unit cost of transporting products across the world.
2. **Technological advances** – cuts the cost of transmitting and communicating information – this is a key factor behind trade in knowledge-intensive products using the latest digital technology.

Continued on next page

3. **Differences in tax systems** - Some nations have cut corporate taxes to attract inflows of foreign direct investment (FDI) as a deliberate strategy to drive growth.
4. **Less protectionism** – average import tariffs have fallen – but in recent years we have seen a rise in non-tariff barriers such as import quotas, domestic subsidies and tougher regulations hinting at a phase of de-globalisation. The average global – or most favoured nation - tariff was 8.9% in 2021 according to the World Trade Organization. In the 1990s and much of the 2000s it was above 8%.

Transnational corporations (TNCs)

Transnational corporations (TNCs) base their manufacturing, assembly, research and retail operations in a number of countries. Many TNCs have become synonymous with globalisation such as Nike, Facebook, Apple, Netflix, Uber, Amazon, Google and Samsung. The biggest 500 TNCs together account for nearly 70% of the value of world trade.

TNCs are a key driver of globalisation because they have been re-locating manufacturing to countries with relatively **lower unit labour costs** to increase profits and returns for shareholders. For example, Volkswagen, Toyota, Nissan and General Motors all have plants in Mexico which has helped Mexico to build a **comparative advantage** in assembling, manufacturing and then exporting vehicles to other countries including the United States and Canada.

A key recent feature of globalisation has been a surge in the number of transnational businesses from **emerging market** / fast-growing developing countries. For example, China Mobile is in the top ten consumer brands in the world and Alibaba has expanded to be the biggest global online retailer. The Tata Group conglomerate from India has made significant investments in Western economies e.g. buying Jaguar Land Rover. Infosys from India is one of the world's biggest information system businesses employing over 160,000 people worldwide.

Impacts of globalisation and global companies

When considering the impact of globalisation, you need to ensure that you think about the impact on individual countries, governments, producers and consumers, workers and the environment.

> **Exam Tip** The impact of globalisation will be different in different countries depending on how well integrated they are in the world economy and also whether they have the factor resources that allow them to gain from globalisation. When evaluating the impacts of globalisation, look at the effects on a case by case basis. Some nations are more open to trade and investment than others and are at different stages of their economic development.

Advantages from globalisation

The transformation of **emerging market economies** in the last 30 years, and the resulting reduction in extreme poverty, have been built on globalisation. That process has helped cut prices and raised living standards in the West. Here are some of the main advantages of globalisation:

1. Globalisation encourages both producers and consumers to reap benefits from the **deeper division of labour** in global supply chains and harness **economies of scale** – leading to gains in economic welfare.
2. More **competitive markets** through trade reduces the level of monopoly supernormal profits and can also incentivise businesses to seek cost-reducing innovations.
3. Trade can help drive faster economic growth which leads to **higher income per head**. This has reduced the extent of extreme poverty in the world economy.
4. There are advantages from the **freer movement of labour** between countries including relieving labour shortages and promoting the sharing of ideas from diverse workforces.
5. Opening up of capital markets such as bond and stock markets increases the opportunities for developing countries to borrow money to help overcome a domestic savings gap.
6. Globalisation has increased awareness among people around the world of the systemic challenge from climate change and the effects of wealth/income inequality.
7. Competitive pressures of globalisation may prompt improved standards of government and better labour protection through improved monitoring by international organisations.

Drawbacks from globalisation

1. Rising inequality / relative poverty: the gains from globalisation will be unequal leading to growing political and social tensions if inequality of income and wealth increases.
2. Threats to the global commons e.g. irreversible damage to ecosystems, land degradation, deforestation, loss of bio-diversity and severe water scarcity from a growing world economy.

3. Globalisation can lead to greater exploitation of the environment, e.g. increased production of raw materials, and the impact of trading toxic waste to countries with weaker environmental laws.
4. Macroeconomic fragility: in an inter-connected world economy, external shocks in one region can rapidly spread to other centres (this is known as systemic risk).
5. Trade imbalances: increasing trade imbalances (both surpluses and deficits) lead to protectionist tensions, wider use of tariffs and quotas and also a move towards managed exchange rates.
6. Workers may suffer structural unemployment as a direct result of the out-sourcing of manufacturing to lower-cost countries and a rise in the share of imports in a nation's GDP.
7. Dominant global brands: businesses with dominant brands and superior technologies may squeeze out smaller local producers leading to a reduction in choice for consumers and some job losses.

Exam Tip Globalisation inevitably creates people who gain and groups who lose out. The overall impact depends on the effectiveness of policies such as environmental interventions and labour market policies designed to help compensate those affected in a harmful way and give people and communities the skills and opportunities required to adjust to a fast-changing world economy.

Impact of globalisation on the UK economy

Has globalisation been of benefit to the UK? It is difficult to make an overall assessment. Many micro and macro aspects can be considered including the following:
- Expanded choice and higher consumer surplus
- Effects on retail prices and the rate of inflation
- Impact of UK firms relocating to lower-wage economies
- Impact of net inward migration on real wages and on UK government spending / tax revenues
- Impact of inward investment into UK on employment
- Impact on share prices and profits of UK companies

The changing world economy
Nearly sixty percent of the value of world GDP now comes from emerging market and developing economies. However, the share of global GDP from sub Saharan Africa is only 3.15 percent.

External shocks in a globalised world

Global Financial Crisis 2007-2009	COVID-19	Volatile world commodity prices	Growth slowdowns in emerging nations
International and regional trade and investment deals	Currency volatility and policy changes e.g. devaluation	Extreme weather events (drought, flooding etc.)	Geo-political uncertainty and risks from terrorism

What are external shocks?
External shocks are events that come from outside a domestic economic system.
- Negative external shocks create instability and can lead to persistent periods of weaker economic growth, higher unemployment, falling real incomes and rising poverty
- External shocks can also be positive e.g. the emergence of and widespread adoption of technologies used by businesses and households in many countries

4.1.2 SPECIALISATION AND TRADE

What you need to know

Absolute and comparative advantage (numerical and diagrammatic analysis needed)

Assumptions and limitations relating to the theory of comparative advantage

Advantages and disadvantages of specialisation and trade in an international context

Absolute advantage

Absolute advantage occurs when a country can supply a product using fewer resources than another nation. If a country using the same factors of production can produce more of a product, then it has an absolute advantage. Consider the following example of 2 people engaged in 2 tasks and splitting their time equally.

Output with both workers having 10 hours of time available		
	Bricks Laid (in 5 hours)	Cakes Baked (in 5 hours)
Harry	40	10
Hermione	20	25
Total (5 hours each)	60 (40 + 20)	35 (10 + 25)

In this example:

- With both people having the same factor resource (time) available
- Harry can lay more bricks than Hermione (80 to 40) in 10 hours
- Hermione can bake more cakes than Harry (50 to 20) in 10 hours
- Harry therefore has the absolute advantage in brick-laying
- Hermione therefore has the absolute advantage in baking cakes
- If they both specialise fully, then total output of bricks and cakes can increase

Output with both workers having 10 hours of time available		
	Bricks Laid	Cakes Baked
Harry	80	0
Hermione	0	50
Total (10 hours each)	80 (a gain of 20)	50 (a gain of 15)

In this example:

We are assuming there are constant returns from specialisation

- Harry specialises in laying bricks by allocating all of his time to the task
- Hermione specialises in baking cakes by allocating all of her time to the task
- Total output of both products increases from applying absolute advantage

Comparative advantage

David Ricardo was one of the founding fathers of **classical economics**. He developed the idea of comparative advantage, which helps to explain why even small countries without an absolute advantage can and do trade. Comparative advantage exists when:

- The **relative opportunity cost of production** for a good or service is lower in one nation than another country
- A country is relatively more **productively efficient** than another
- The basic rule is to **specialise** your scarce resources in the goods and services that you are relatively best at
- This opens up gains from specialisation and trade which then leads to a more **efficient allocation of resources**

Worked Example
of comparative advantage and potential gains from specialisation and trade

Output with ½ of all available resources allocated to each industry in both countries

	Beef	Tobacco	Opportunity Cost Ratio of beef & tobacco
Australia	250	200	5:4
Malawi	100	150	2:3
Total	350	350	

Ratios are an important quantitative skill

Australia has a comparative advantage in producing beef. This is because the opportunity cost of an extra unit of beef is 4/5th unit of tobacco, whereas for Malawi the opportunity cost is 1½ units of tobacco.
- i.e. Australia needs to give up less tobacco to produce more beef than Malawi does

Malawi has a comparative advantage in producing tobacco – the opportunity cost of an extra unit of tobacco is 2/3rd of beef whereas for Australia it is 1¼.
- i.e. Malawi needs to give up less beef to produce more tobacco than Australia does

Here's what happens if the countries choose to specialise in the good in which they have a comparative advantage:

Output after specialisation has taken place

	Beef	Tobacco
Australia	400 (+150)	80 (-120)
Malawi	0 (-100)	300 (+150)
Total	400 (+50)	380 (+30)

If both countries specialise according to the law of comparative advantage, and **assuming constant returns to scale**, then total output of both products (beef and tobacco) can rise. In this particular example, because Australia's economy is so much larger than Malawi's, Australia will continue to produce some tobacco so that total world output does not decline following specialisation.

Extension idea

Output after trade has taken place

	Beef	Tobacco
Australia	270	210
Malawi	130	170
Total	400	380

If both countries trade at a **mutually** beneficial terms of trade of 1 beef for 1 tobacco – they can both end up with more of both products – this is a gain in economic welfare. As a result, Australia exports 130 units of beef and then trades for 130 units of tobacco with Malawi, i.e. the terms of trade are set at 1:1.

Assumptions behind the theory of comparative advantage and trade

Key assumptions behind the theory are as follows:
1. **Constant returns to scale** i.e. no economies of scale which might in reality amplify the gains from trade
2. **Perfect factor mobility** between industries (e.g. geographical and occupational mobility of labour)
3. **No trade barriers** such as tariffs and quotas which artificially change the prices at which trade occurs
4. **Low transportation costs** to get products to market – high logistics costs might erode comparative advantage
5. **No significant externalities** from production and/or consumption of the products being traded

Furthermore, the model is a simplistic 2-country 2-product model, which in itself is unrealistic.

⭐ **Exam Tip** The comparative advantage model is simplistic and may not reflect the real world (for example, only two countries are taken into account). Most exports contain inputs from many different countries and products can travel across borders many times before a finished good or service is made available for sale to consumers. Businesses rather than countries trade (as a general rule).

⭐ **Exam Tip** Mutually beneficial terms of trade are not necessarily those that benefit both countries equally – the benefits from exporting and importing goods and services may be unbalanced. Indeed, the perceived unfairness of trade is often used as one justification for protectionist policies such as import tariffs and quotas and forms of hidden protectionism. Whenever you are discussing the economics of trade, remember to comment on possible distributional effects as part of the evaluation.

Advantages of specialisation and trade

Most economists argue that trade in goods and services across national borders is an important driver of increased competition and innovation and therefore helpful in sustaining growth and improving living standards. However, it is important to be aware of some of the risks and drawbacks if a country becomes more open to international trade.

Gains from trade – an overview

1. Free trade allows for deeper specialisation and benefits from economies of scale (increasing returns)
2. Free trade increases market competition and choice and also drives up product quality for consumers
3. Increased market contestability reduces prices for consumers leading to higher real incomes
4. Trade can lead to a better use of scarce resources for example from trade in sustainable technologies

Trade and economic efficiency

It is important in your analysis to link some of the potential gains from trade to different types of economic efficiency.

Economic efficiency	Possible impact of trade on economic efficiency
Allocative efficiency	Competition from lower-cost import sources drives market prices down closer to marginal cost and then reduces the level of monopoly (supernormal) profits
Productive efficiency	Specialising and selling in larger markets encourages increasing returns to scale (economies of scale) i.e. a lower long run average cost of production
Dynamic efficiency	Economies open to trade may see more innovative businesses which invest more in research and development and also in the human capital of their workforce to help raise labour productivity
X-inefficiency	Intense competition in markets provides a discipline on businesses to keep their unit costs under control to remain price competitive and profitable

Gains from trade using supply and demand analysis

In this example we consider how consumers and producers might be affected by the ability to import coal into the EU at an import-tariff free price which is lower than domestic suppliers can offer. Opening up a country to trade has welfare effects for producers, consumers, employees, the government and other stakeholders.

If coal can be imported at a lower price, consumer surplus increases but producer surplus for coal producers in the EU falls because they can no longer sell their output at the previous high price.

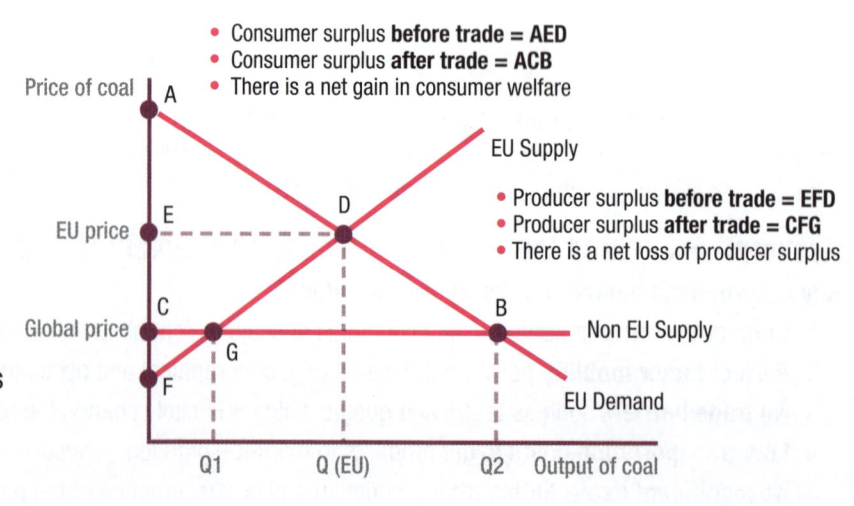

- Consumer surplus **before trade = AED**
- Consumer surplus **after trade = ACB**
- There is a net gain in consumer welfare

- Producer surplus **before trade = EFD**
- Producer surplus **after trade = CFG**
- There is a net loss of producer surplus

8 Edexcel A Level Economics Theme 4 Study Book

Drawbacks of specialisation and trade

| Transport costs e.g. carbon emissions from increased food miles | Negative externalities from both production and consumption | Risk of rising structural unemployment as trade patterns change | 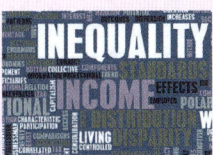 Inequality – benefits from globalisation are unequally shared | Pressure on real wages to fall in advanced and emerging countries | Risks from global shocks such as the Global Financial Crisis and COVID-19 |

Some of the main risks / drawbacks are summarised below:
1. Volatile global prices affecting export revenues and profits for producers and tax revenues for governments
2. Risks that exports will be affected by geo-political uncertainties and cyclical fluctuations in demand
3. Opening up to trade and investment may cause rising structural unemployment in some industries as the pattern of demand, output and jobs changes. Poorer countries may opt instead for a strategy of industrialisation aided by import protectionism before they eventually open up their markets
4. Countries that specialise in only a few primary commodities may suffer from the natural resource trap (also known as the resource curse) which may make them poorer than countries less dependent on exporting primary commodities – this is covered in more detail later in this study book.

> **Exam Tip** It can be a very good idea to learn a 2 x 2 matrix to show comparative advantage, as it can be difficult under exam timed pressure to come up with a brand-new example!

> **Exam Tip** Make sure that you can work out opportunity cost and therefore comparative advantage from both numbers in a table and a PPF diagram. You may need to revisit Theme 1 to remind yourself of PPFs.

4.1.3 PATTERN OF TRADE

What you need to know

Factors influencing the pattern of trade between countries and changes in trade flows between countries:
- Comparative advantage
- Impact of emerging economies
- Growth of trading blocs and bilateral trading agreements
- Changes in relative exchange rates

What is the geographical pattern of trade?
- This is the countries with whom businesses and people trade
- Intra-regional trade is trade between countries in the same region (European Union, Africa, Asia)
  - Note that this is different from **inter-regional trade**, which is trade **between** different regions i.e. between Europe and N America
- Countries tend to trade most with other nations in closest proximity

Geographical pattern of trade for the UK (2024 data)

	Country	% of Total Imports from	% of Total Exports to
1	China	12.4%	7.54%
2	Germany	10.2%	8.66%
3	United States	10.1%	13.2%
4	Netherlands	5.11%	8.93%
5	France	4.7%	6.43%
6	Ireland	2.54%	6.94%

Other patterns of trade

Many less economically developed countries rely heavily on primary product exports. Some less developed countries have a high level of primary product dependence – here are some examples:

- Angola: 72.9% of exports is crude petroleum (oil), 9.28% is diamonds
- Ethiopia: 36.5% of exports is coffee
- Zambia: 63.3% of exports is raw copper, refined copper and cobalt
- Kenya: 18.9% of exports is tea and 9.06% cut flowers

The pattern of trade changes as countries move through **different stages of development**. As a nation develops thus increasing **complexity** and **capabilities**, then they become capable of supplying and then exporting a broader range of products within the global economy. A really good example of this over the last forty years is South Korea.

Often the transition to a different pattern of trade comes from switching from growing and extracting to processing and refining primary products through to final assembly and manufacturing. Patterns of trade also adjust as countries develop a new comparative advantage in industries such as financial services, transportation and tourism. The emergence of a more diverse pattern of trade requires significant investment in human as well as physical capital.

Trade in goods

Goods exported and imported include commodities, and tangible manufactured products such as cars, components for aircraft, processed food and drink, chemicals, pharmaceuticals, steel and computer equipment. Over 70 per cent of merchandise exports (globally) are manufactured goods.

Trade in services

Heavily traded services include transportation (freight and passengers), tourism, health and education services, financial services such as foreign exchange dealing and a huge range of business services such as accountancy, consultancy, design and marketing. Services include computer and information services, royalties and license fees. There has been a huge growth in international trade in services over the last thirty years. Many countries now export creative services such as TV series, film rights, and other cultural events.

Factors affecting comparative advantage and patterns of trade

Comparative advantage is a **dynamic concept** it changes over time as a result of adjustments in:

1. The quantity and quality of natural resources available e.g. the discovery of new mineral reserves
2. Demographics – factors such as an ageing population, net migration, women's participation in the labour force
3. Rates of new capital investment including infrastructure spending
4. Investment in research and development (R&D) which can drive business innovation
5. Fluctuations in the exchange rate which then affect the relative prices of exports and imports
6. Import controls such as tariffs, export subsidies and quotas used to create an artificial comparative advantage
7. Non-price competitiveness e.g. product design, innovation, product reliability, branding, technical standards

The impact of emerging economies on trade patterns

An emerging economy is one that can't yet be classified as 'developed', and is investing heavily in its productive capacity.
The 4 largest emerging economies (in terms of GDP at PPP) are still the BRICs, that is, Brazil, Russia, India and China. We can also consider the CIVETS (Colombia, Indonesia, Vietnam, Egypt, Turkey and South Africa) and the MINT economies (Mexico, Indonesia, Nigeria and Turkey). Emerging economies can impact on trade patterns in the following ways:

- Rising income means that they start to purchase more goods/services from elsewhere in the world, over and above basic necessities e.g. demand for imported milk in China
    - This can also include increasing imports of commodities, which can push up prices of commodities for others
- Attract MNC activity, as well as grow their own large companies which start to operate elsewhere in the world:
    - Examples include: Huawei and China Construction Bank from China, Tata from India, and Petrobas from Brazil
- Selling more medium to high value exports e.g. manufactured items and electronics, rather than commodities or low-value-added items
- Currency volatility in emerging markets can have a large impact on commodity prices and raw material prices in other countries
- Rising tension between developed economies e.g. US and emerging economies such as China, resulting in trade wars / protectionist measures, as each country seeks a bigger slice of the world trading pie

The impact of trade blocs and bilateral trading agreements on trade patterns

A trade bloc consists of a number of countries that agree to trade with each other with reduced or no trade barriers (such as tariffs or quotas). There are varying degrees of integration and types of trade bloc:

- Preferential trade area – there is reduced protectionism on a number of select goods/services amongst the countries involved
    - This could just be between 2 countries i.e. **bilateral**
- Free trade area – there is completely free trade between the countries involved, but each country can set their own trade restrictions on countries outside of the agreement
    - Examples include USMCA and EFTA
- Customs Union – there is completely free trade between the countries involved **and** they all agree to impose the same trade restrictions on other countries outside their bloc
    - Examples include MERCOSUR (S America) and Turkey's relationship with the EU

One key impact of the increase in the number and strength of trading blocs on global trading patterns is that they often lead to more intra-regional trade (i.e. **within** the trade bloc itself) and less inter-regional trade (i.e. trade **between** regions / blocs). This may mean that countries do not always gain the benefits from specialising according to their comparative advantage. There may be **trade creation** at the expense of **trade diversion**.

The impact of changes in relative exchange rates on trade patterns

An exchange rate is simply the price of one currency in terms of another. Some countries operate floating exchange rates, where the price of the currency is determined entirely by demand and supply on the foreign exchange market. Other countries operate fixed or pegged exchange rate systems, where the price is determined by the government or monetary authorities, who then conduct policy (e.g. manipulating interest rates or buying/selling currency) to maintain that rate. A strong currency (i.e. one that requires a lot of other currencies to buy it) makes exports appear relatively more expensive and imports appear relatively cheaper. A weak currency (i.e. one that does not require a lot of other currencies to buy it) makes exports appear relatively cheap and imports relatively expensive. Clearly, exchange rates can therefore affect the pattern of trade.

> **Data in focus**
> In August 2019, the US Treasury officially declared that China was a 'currency manipulator', after the Chinese currency dropped in value against the US dollar unexpectedly, reaching its lowest value since 2007. At a time when tensions between the two countries in relation to trade were already high, the movement of the Chinese currency was not welcomed by the US government, which claims that slow growth in US export industries is due to 'unfair tactics' by China. China responded to the accusation by saying that its currency was weakening because it was exporting fewer goods as a result of protectionist measures implemented by the US.

> **COMMON ERROR ALERT!**
> Remember that a currency can be weak against one currency but strong against others – it is important to consider relative exchange rates, or even the 'Effective Exchange Rate', which measures the value of a country's currency against a basket of other currencies.

4.1.4 TERMS OF TRADE

What you need to know

Calculation of the terms of trade

Factors influencing a country's terms of trade

Impact of changes in a country's terms of trade

What are the terms of trade?
- The **terms of trade** (ToT) measures the relative prices of a country's exports compared to the prices of imported goods and services
- Terms of trade is the ratio of the weighted price index for exports to the price index for imports

Formula for calculating the terms of trade:

Terms of Trade (ToT) index = (price index for exports) / (price index for imports) x 100

The terms of trade can be interpreted in words as the amount of imported goods and services an economy can purchase per unit of exported goods and services. A rise in the price index for exports of goods and services improves the terms of trade and this means that a country can buy more imports for any given level of exports.

Terms of trade is just one measure of a country's trade competitiveness – another is relative unit labour cost.

An **improvement in the terms of trade** means that export prices are rising relative to import prices. This can be confusing because more expensive exports suggests that demand for exports will decline, thus reducing AD. But, economists say that the ToT has improved when export prices rise because fewer goods have to be exported to buy a certain amount of imports.

Factors influencing the terms of trade
- Global (world) prices for raw materials and components
  - Rising oil prices improve terms of trade for oil exporters
  - Rising gas prices worsen terms of trade for energy importers
- The exchange rate
  - A stronger currency lowers import prices leading to improved terms of trade
- A weaker currency increases import prices leading to reduced terms of trade

- Import tariffs and other trade barriers such as quotas
  - An import tariff (tax) increases the price of imports, other factors remaining the same and this worsens the terms of trade
- Domestic and global inflation rates
- Changing factor endowments

Analysing and evaluating the effects of an improved terms of trade

Cause of improved Terms of Trade	Basic analysis	Evaluation point
A fall in the relative prices of imported technology	This gives a country the chance to import capital goods more cheaply which will then help to increase labour productivity and their long-run competitiveness	Capital-intensive production e.g. using robotics may not necessarily create many new jobs and extra incomes
A rise in the unit export prices of a country's exports	Rising export prices cause an increase in revenues from exports. This is an injection into the circular flow and improves the balance of payments on current account. It also increases the stock of foreign exchange reserves	There is a risk of demand-pull inflation from a surge in export revenues. Inflation hits hardest lower income families i.e. it has a regressive effect on the distribution of income

4.1.5 TRADING BLOCS AND THE WORLD TRADE ORGANIZATION (WTO)

What you need to know

Types of trading blocs (regional trade agreements and bilateral trade agreements):
- Free trade areas
- Customs unions
- Common markets
- Monetary unions: conditions necessary for their success with particular reference to the **Eurozone**

Costs and benefits of regional trade agreements

Role of the WTO in trade liberalisation

Possible conflicts between regional trade agreements and the WTO

Regional Trade Blocs

The **World Trade Organization** (WTO) permits trade blocs, provided that they result in **lower import protection** against outside countries than existed before the creation of the trade bloc. Examples of regional trade blocs include:

1. **USMCA** - United States-Mexico-Canada agreement (which replaced NAFTA in 2018)
2. **Mercosur** – Brazil, Argentina, Uruguay, Paraguay and Venezuela
3. Association of Southeast Asian Nations Free Trade Area – known as **ASEAN**
4. **Common Market of Eastern and Southern Africa** includes Zambia, Rwanda, Eswatini, Ethiopia and Kenya
5. **Trans-Pacific Partnership** (TPP) – an agreement negotiated between Australia, Brunei, Chile, Canada, Malaysia, Mexico, New Zealand, Peru, Singapore and Vietnam (the USA under Trump dropped out)

Free Trade Areas

A **free trade area** (FTA) is where there are **no import tariffs or quotas** on products from one country entering another.

Current examples of free trade areas include:
- **EFTA:** European Free Trade Association consists of Norway, Iceland, Switzerland and Liechtenstein
- **USMCA**: revised trade agreement between the USA, Mexico and Canada
- **South Asian Free Trade Area** between Afghanistan, Bangladesh, Bhutan, India, Maldives, Nepal, Pakistan and Sri Lanka
- **African Continental Free Trade Area**: new agreement with 55 nations
- **Pacific Alliance**: Chile, Colombia, Mexico and Peru

Bilateral trading agreement

A bilateral trade is the exchange of goods **between two economies / groups of economies** promoting trade in goods and services and flows of foreign investment. The two countries will reduce or eliminate import tariffs, import quotas, export restraints, and other non-tariff trade barriers to encourage trade and investment. Examples of bilateral agreements include:
- EU-Japan Economic Partnership Agreement
- ASEAN – China Free Trade Area
- EU-South Korea Free Trade Deal
- China-Australia Free Trade Agreement

African Continental Free Trade Area

In 2018, over 40 African countries signed the **African Continental Free Trade Area**, which aims to accelerate economic integration in Africa and increase trade within the continent. In 2016, intra-Africa trade grew to 19 per cent of Africa's trade, up from 15 percent in 2014. This is significantly higher than the 10 per cent share of intra-Africa trade in 2008.

Chain of reasoning: Examine how a free trade area might stimulate economic growth in sub-Saharan Africa.

A free trade agreement can - in theory – lead to faster economic growth because it encourages nations and businesses to **specialise** and then trade on the basis of their developed **comparative advantage**.	The absence of import tariffs and other barriers **reduces the costs of trading goods and services** across borders. E.g. Kenya may trade more with Ethiopia – this is known as **intra-regional trade** and is low within Sub Saharan Africa.	**As a result,** the **prices** of traded goods and services are likely to fall since trade stimulates increased **competition** and can therefore cause improvements in **labour productivity** and also helps businesses to achieve **internal economies of scale**.
This means that the free trade agreement could cause a rise in **capital spending** which will then cause an outward shift of **long run aggregate supply**. In this way, countries involved may see an increase in their **potential growth rate**.	**A likely effect of this** is to stimulate increased output which will then lead to an increase in the demand for labour (a **derived demand**) and also capital investment e.g. in **trade infrastructure** such as new ports and better roads.	**This leads to** an increase in the **real incomes of consumers** which then means that they can afford to **increase demand and consumption**. Lower prices are a **welfare gain** for consumers. Overall this is **trade creation**.

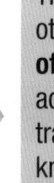

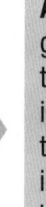

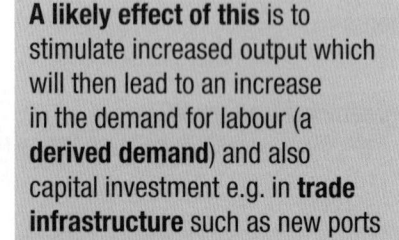

Evaluation approaches to the impact of the new African Continental Free Trade Area:

Theory focuses on welfare gains:	Lower prices for consumers Economies of scale for suppliers Increased competition in markets Improved allocative efficiency i.e. a gain in economic efficiency
Evaluation	Lost tariff revenues for national governments Financing costs for building the necessary trade infrastructure Regulatory reforms for common product standards will add costs for businesses Local SME's may suffer a loss of profit / jobs when facing stronger competition

Customs Unions

A customs union comprises a group of countries that agree to
- **Abolish tariffs** and quotas between member nations to encourage free movement of goods and services.
- Adopt a **common external tariff** on imports from non-member countries. In the case of the EU, the tariff imposed on, say, imports of South Korean TV screens will be the same in every EU country.
- Preferential tariff rates apply to trade agreements that the European Union has entered into with third countries or groupings of third countries.

The **EU** is a customs union. The EU also has customs union agreements with Turkey, Andorra and San Marino. Another example of a customs union is the **South African Customs Union** involving Botswana, Lesotho, Namibia, South Africa, Eswatini. Another is the **Eurasian Customs Union** involving Armenia, Belarus, Kazakhstan, Kyrgyzstan and Russia.

How does a trading bloc differ from a customs union?

- A trading bloc is essentially an agreement between countries to lower their import tariffs and perhaps extend this to reducing the use of non-tariff barriers to trade. In a free trade area, each country continues to be able to set their own distinct external tariff on goods imported from the rest of the world.
- A customs union is different from a free trade area, in which no tariffs are charged on goods and services moving within the area. It adds on a **common external tariff** (CET) on all products flowing from countries outside the customs union, unless specific trade deals have been established. Revenues from import tariffs are combined for all member states. The countries in a customs union negotiate as a bloc when discussing trade deals with countries outside the union. A good example is the recently introduced bilateral trade deal between the European Union and Japan.

Common (Single) Markets

Common markets represent a **deeper integration** between participating countries. They usually extend beyond free trade in goods and services to include free movement of labour across borders and the relaxation of capital controls.

Ways in which a Customs Union differs from a Single Market

- A single market is a stronger and deeper form of integration than a customs union.
- A single market involves the free movement of goods and services, capital and labour.
- In addition to a common external tariff, a single market also tries to cut back on the use of non-tariff barriers such as different rules on product safety and environmental standards replacing them with a **common set of rules** governing trade in goods and services within the common market.

Countries such as Norway and Switzerland are outside of the EU, but they are members of the EU single market, paying into the EU budget to take advantage of some of the benefits of the free flow of capital, labour, goods and services.

The EU single market is built on four key freedoms:

1. **Free trade in goods**: businesses can sell their products anywhere in EU member states and consumers can buy where they want with no penalty
2. **Mobility of labour**: citizens of EU states can live, study and work in any other EU country
3. **Free movement of capital:** financial capital can flow freely between member states and EU citizens can use financial services such as insurance in any EU state.
4. **Free trade in services**: services such as pensions, architectural services, telecoms and advertising can be offered in any EU member state.

The most recent country to join the European Union was Croatia. The United Kingdom voted to leave the EU in a referendum held in June 2016 which subsequently triggered the Brexit process after Article 50 was invoked.

Potential economic benefits from countries joining the EU single market:

Possible advantage	Comment
Import-tariff free access to a single market of nearly 500 million people	Opportunity to exploit economies of scale – lower long run average costs
Easier to access foreign direct investment from inside/outside the EU	Inward FDI can lift trend growth and raise factor productivity
Access to EU structural funds – made available to poorer EU nations	Investment helps improve infrastructure and potential output
Better access to EU capital markets	EU companies can raise investment funds from bond and capital markets
Discipline of intense competition from being inside the EU single market	Businesses must become more cost efficient + improve dynamic efficiency

Monetary Union

- Monetary union is a form of economic integration beyond participation in a single market
- The single European currency was introduced in 1999 and came into common circulation in January 2002
- No country has yet left the Euro Area despite the problems
- As of July 2024, there are 20 member nations
- Countries not part of the single currency include Denmark and Poland

Possible advantages from joining the single currency

Joining the single currency is a significant economic and political choice and one that countries will make only after assessing the likely longer-term benefits and risks involved.

Currency risk	Trade	Investment	Competition	Transactions
Euro is more stable than smaller currencies. Reduced currency risk makes it easier for smaller countries to borrow money	Euro enhances the gains from being in the single market – e.g. it encourages more cross border trade in goods and services	Membership of Euro is likely to stimulate inward investment e.g. in industries such as tourism, financial services, car-making	Euro increases price transparency and market competition which then helps consumers to find products at better prices	A shared currency eliminates the costly conversion of money, it might also improve labour mobility within the EU single market

There are however **risks and drawbacks** from committing to joining a single currency:

- A country's central bank loses the freedom to set monetary policy interest rates solely to meet macro objectives such as lowering inflation (higher interest rates) or preventing a recession (lower interest rates).
- Joining a common currency means that the option of a managed depreciation / devaluation of the exchange rate to help improve price competitiveness in overseas markets is also lost. Instead to become more price competitive, a government may have to maintain deflationary fiscal policies to achieve an internal devaluation of the price level.
- There are also **adjustment costs** when switching currencies including **menu costs** and the risk that some retailers will increase prices when the currency is switched to make extra profit in the short term.

Conditions necessary for the success of a monetary union

These conditions are associated with the concept of an optimal currency area (OCA). An OCA works best when:
- Countries are **highly integrated** i.e. a high percentage of trade is with fellow currency union nations. A good example is Slovenia. Well over 80 percent of their trade is done with fellow members of the Euro Zone.
- Each economy has a **flexible labour market** to cope with external shocks. Flexibility might include:
  - Flexibility in real wages and salaries during an economic cycle
  - Workers with adaptable skills to reduce the risk of structural unemployment
  - High geographical mobility within and between countries
  - Flexible employment contracts including short-term job contracts
- The effects of interest rate changes or a movement in the exchange rate have a broadly similar effect on businesses and households from country to country.
- Nations are willing to make **fiscal transfers** between each other and provide financial support during difficult economic times.

The Euro Zone is a long way from being an optimal currency area. The nineteen member nations have many differences in their patterns of trade and in the structure of their economies. Consider for example contrasts between Germany (one of the world's biggest exporters of manufactured goods) with Spain (which is more reliant on construction, finance and tourism). There are sizeable differences in per capita incomes throughout the Euro Area and big differences too in the structure of housing finance and in labour productivity. All of this has made it tricky for the European Central Bank (ECB) to set a successful "one size fits all" interest rate that suits the interests of participating countries.

The economic crisis that engulfed Greece is a good example of the perils of joining a single currency when the country was unused to low interest rates, too willing to increase their household and government debt and suffering from a lack of price and non-price competitiveness with established (and richer) EU nations.

Costs and benefits of regional trade agreements

One major benefit from regional trade agreements between countries that lower tariffs and abolish quotas and other barriers to trade is that it can lead to **trade creation** effects.

Trade creation occurs when countries agree a trade deal that lowers tariffs between them (this may extend to a formal customs union). As a result of a reduced tariff, consumers in a participating nation can now source imports from a lower cost country which leads to lower prices and a rise in real incomes. Trade creation can be illustrated using a trade liberalisation diagram.

But the expanding number of regional trade agreements can also be seen as a threat to globalisation. The WTO has noted a trend towards regionalisation of trade for example within East Asia or the European Union. Some of the world's poorest countries might not be able to negotiate favourable tariff or quota free access to many of the markets of rich, advanced countries. The WTO would prefer a **global trade deal** covering many goods and services rather than the complex patchwork quilt of having over 4,000 separate free trade deals across the global economy in 2018.

Role of the WTO in trade liberalisation

The World Trade Organization (WTO) was founded in 1995, but had its origins in the 1947 General Agreement on Trade and Tariffs (GATT). A key principle of the WTO is that of multilateral trade. The WTO describes itself as having 4 roles: conductor, tribunal, monitor and trainer. The WTO believes that:

"Global rules of trade provide assurance and stability. Consumers and producers know they can enjoy secure supplies and greater choice of the finished products, components, raw materials and services they use. Producers and exporters know foreign markets will remain open to them"

Conductor role

Members of the WTO have come up with a set of rules that apply to international trade; the WTO ensures that these rules are followed. The WTO organises 'rounds' of negotiations to be able to develop new rules (e.g. in response to the rise of trade in services), but these can take well over a decade to be agreed upon, as there needs to be a consensus amongst members. The latest round is known as the Doha round, and was launched in 2001. Any agreements reached are then ratified by domestic parliaments.

Tribunal role

This role involves settling disputes between members. Members are encouraged to sort out disputes by themselves, but occasionally the WTO needs to convene a panel of experts.

Monitor role
The WTO reviews the trade policies of its members to make sure that WTO rules are being applied fairly and consistently.

Training role
The WTO provides training to government officials in (mostly) developing countries, to help them engage in trade with other WTO members.

Conflicts between trade blocs and the WTO
Trade blocs engage in free trade with their members (which is in line with WTO aims) but often put up trade restrictions / barriers against non-members (which is against WTO aims). All WTO members are also currently members of at least 1 regional trade agreement (RTA).

The WTO has said that regional trade agreements can, however, often support the WTO's aims. Agreements on a local or regional scale often go beyond what might have been possible in multilateral trade discussions, and can pave the way for new policies to be rolled out to all WTO members. Agreements on intellectual property, environmental protection and investment at regional level have informed WTO discussion on a multilateral level.

The WTO allows regional trade agreements provided that certain criteria are met. In particular, trade should flow more freely within the RTA without barriers being raised on countries external to the RTA. Furthermore, developed countries are allowed to give special trade treatment, in some circumstances, to developing countries. In the words of the WTO "regional integration should complement the multilateral trading system and not threaten it". If this principle is not upheld, the WTO believes that RTA's violate its key principle of the **most-favoured nation** (i.e. any special favour granted to one country must be granted to all, to avoid discrimination).

4.1.6 RESTRICTIONS ON FREE TRADE

> **What you need to know**
>
> Reasons for restrictions on free trade
>
> Types of restrictions on trade:
> - Import tariffs
> - Subsidies to domestic producers
> - Import quotas
> - Non-tariff barriers
>
> Impact of protectionist policies on consumers, producers, governments, living standards and equality

> **Exam Tip** Most students in exam questions on protectionism focus their answers on import tariffs. The best students recognise that there are **many types of trade restriction** and they make a clear distinction between **tariff and non-tariff barriers**. There are many subtle forms of trade restriction, sometimes known as "hidden protectionism" and it is a good idea to have some applied examples of these in your study notes ahead of an exam.

What are the main reasons for protectionism?
The key justifications for protectionism include:

1. **Infant industry argument** – protecting emerging industries until they have achieved economies of scale
2. **Sunset industry argument** – use tariffs to slow the decline of old sectors and limit structural unemployment
3. **Diversify an economy** thought to be too dependent on one product (e.g. primary product dependence)
4. **Raise tax revenues** - this is important for many developing countries with a limited domestic tax base
5. **Improve the trade balance** and preserve jobs in key industries
6. **Prevention of unfair trade practices such as import dumping** – where excess output is sold in another country at a price below costs of production
7. **Protect strategic industries** – these might include national defence, electricity generation, supply of basic foodstuffs
8. Protectionism can be a **retaliatory response** to another country's policies, for example, poor environmental or labour standards

Import dumping and the case for protectionism
- Dumping happens when firms sell exports at below costs or below normal prices in the home market.
  - The former implies **predatory pricing** – which is illegal
  - The latter implies a strategy of **price discrimination** – this is not illegal
- A topical recent example is the global steel industry. China's steel industry is experiencing significant excess capacity and China has been accused of dumping its steel products on the European Union, selling them for less than they are worth. That makes it harder for EU steel producers to compete.
- Anti-dumping duties (or tariffs) raise the price of a product to help protect local producers.

Anti-dumping tariffs are allowed under WTO rules when cases of dumping have been established. There are three main options when introducing an anti-dumping import duty:

1. **An ad valorem duty** – % of the net EU frontier price. This is the most common import duty.
2. **A specific duty** – a fixed value e.g. $100 per tonne of a product.
3. **A variable duty** – a minimum import price (MIP). Importers in the EU do not pay an anti-dumping duty if the foreign exporter's export price to the EU is higher than the MIP. The lesser-duty rule is that duties can't exceed the level needed to repair the harm done to European industry by the unfair dumping practices – currently between 9-13% for a range of steel products imported into the EU from China.

Types of trade restriction

Protectionist policy	Brief definition
Import quota	A physical limit on the quantity of a good that can be imported into a country
Import tariff	A tax on imports that may be ad valorem (%) or a specific tax (a set amount per unit imported)
Non-tariff barrier	Trade barriers such as import quotas, environmental regulations, trade embargoes and export subsidies
Rules of origin	Rules on the national source of a product e.g. a country might set a minimum percentage for locally-sourced components
Subsidy	Payments by the government to suppliers that reduce their costs; the effect of a subsidy is to increase supply and therefore reduce the market equilibrium price

Import tariffs – analysis and evaluation of impact

Import tariffs are taxes on imports and they aim to protect domestic suppliers from overseas competition by increasing the relative price of imports in the home market thereby causing a switch of spending towards domestic producers. Import tariffs also generate tax revenues for the government and may – over time – lead to an improvement in a nation's trade balance.

Summary of the likely impact of an import tariff

	Impact of an import tariff	Comment
Domestic output	Expansion	Higher price from the import tariff incentivises expansion of output
Domestic demand	Contraction	Higher price reduces the number that are willing to pay for the product
Imports	Fall in volume	Tariff causes expenditure switching towards domestic production
Government tax revenues	Increase	Tariff revenue generates revenue for the government
Domestic producer revenue	Increase	A rise in producer surplus
Foreign producer revenue	Falls	They are selling fewer exports after the tariff – their revenue contracts
Consumer surplus	Falls	Consumers hit by higher prices
Overall economic welfare	Falls	There is a deadweight loss of welfare / loss of economic efficiency

Tariff analysis diagrams:

1 Diagram before a tariff is applied to imported steel:

P1 is the domestic equilibrium price for steel in the market

At the world price PW, domestic demand (Q3) is higher than domestic supply (Q2) – the resulting gap is made up by importing steel at price PW

If there is free trade, then steel will be traded at the world price (PW)

Quantity of imported steel = Q2Q3

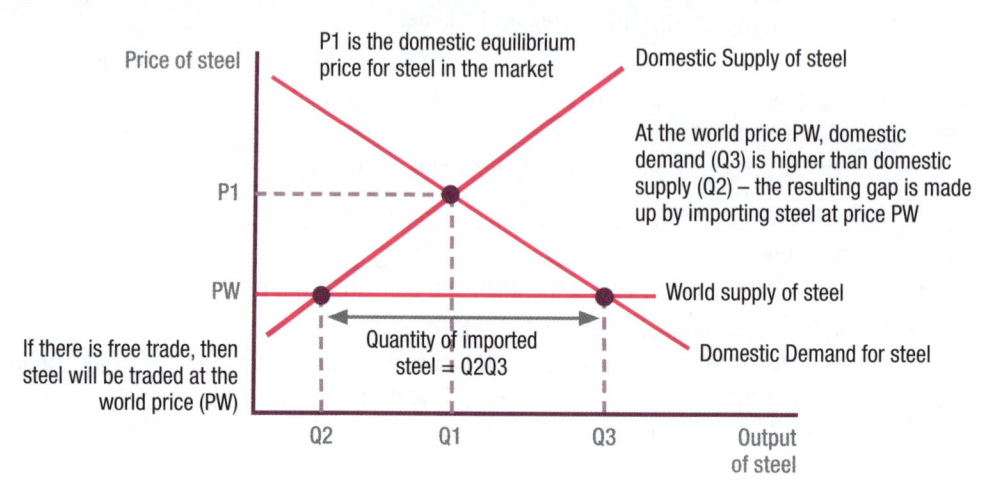

2 Diagram after a tariff is applied to imported steel

A tariff increases the price at which steel is traded by shifting the world supply to PW + tariff

At the higher price after the tariff, domestic demand contracts to Q4 and domestic supply expands to Q5

As a result of the import tariff, the quantity of imports decreases to (Q5-Q4)

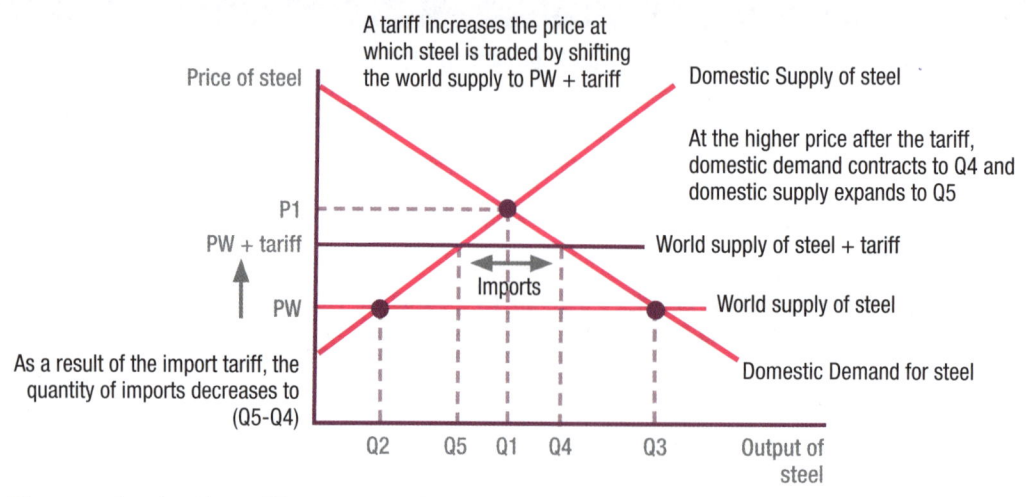

3 Diagram showing the tariff tax revenue for the government

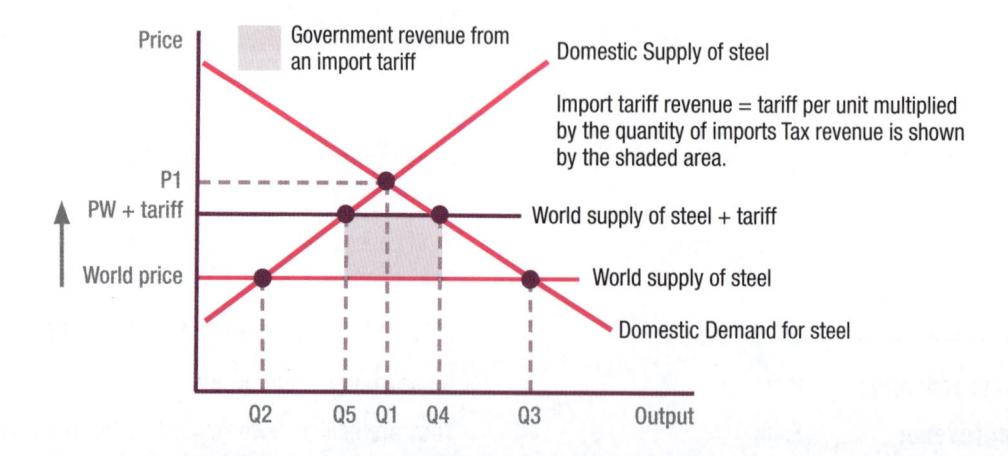

Government revenue from an import tariff

Import tariff revenue = tariff per unit multiplied by the quantity of imports Tax revenue is shown by the shaded area.

Exam Tip Keep up to date with news on trade wars / trade disputes between countries – this will give you excellent awareness to use in the exams!

20 **Edexcel A Level Economics Theme 4 Study Book**

Import Quotas

- A quota is a limit on the total quantity of a product can be supplied to a market
- An import quota therefore restricts supply of an imported product
- By cutting market supply, the price of the imported product is likely to rise
- Black markets may develop with agents trading at unofficial prices

	Impact of an import quota	Comment
Domestic output	Increases	A higher price makes it more profitable for domestic suppliers to enter the market
Domestic demand	Contracts	Because the quota reduces the quantity of cheap imports available
Import volumes	Contracts	Reduction in quantity depends on how severe (low) is the import cap
Tax revenues	No direct effect	A quota is different from an import tariff
Domestic producer revenue	Increases	Selling increased output at higher price
Foreign producer revenue	Falls	Quota caps how much can be exported into the protected market
Consumer surplus	Falls	Higher prices reduce consumer welfare
Overall welfare	Falls	Quota restricts free trade and leads to deadweight loss of economic welfare

Impact of an import quota on different stakeholders

	Impact	Evaluation
Domestic producers	Domestic producers benefit from the cap on imports – this increases the market price and makes it more profitable for them to stay in / enter the market.	Quota is a barrier to trade, might encourage domestic firms to become less productively efficient. Some producers hampered by scarce supply of higher quality overseas imports – hurts their competitiveness.
Consumers	Consumers likely to face a higher price in the market because of limit on import products. Less competition in the market might also affect the quality of products available – impact on utility.	Consumers who work for domestic firms may benefit from higher employment and wages. Import cap might stimulate increased investment in alternatives.
The government	Improved external balance from the reduction in imports and an expansion of GDP from the increase in domestic production.	No immediate tax revenues from an import quota - a contrast with an import tariff.

Domestic (and export) subsidies

What is a domestic subsidy?

- A domestic subsidy is any form of government financial help to domestic businesses
- The subsidy helps firms to lower their costs and thus become more competitive in home and overseas markets
- Export subsidies are financial incentives to sell products in overseas markets at a profit

	Impact on analysis	Evaluation
Domestic producers	Domestic producers gain from the subsidy – they get the world price + a subsidy payment. Higher revenues will lift profits and might therefore lead to a higher share price. Increased output creates the possibility of economies of scale.	Risk of a dependency culture emerging – i.e. businesses relying on the subsidies rather than taking their own steps to become more competitive by increasing productivity, eliminating inefficiency and accelerating the pace of process/product innovation.
Consumers	Assuming that the subsidy is not large enough to change the world price, no direct effect on the prices that consumers pay for their products.	They may face higher taxes if expensive subsidies take up a high percentage of government spending.
The government	Subsidy can be an effective non-tariff barrier to reduce the volume of imports by encouraging domestic production.	Unlike a tariff, a subsidy does not generate tax revenues directly. Increased spending on subsidies may then cause a growing budget deficit.

Non-tariff barriers (NTBs)

There are many different types of **non-tariff barrier** – some of the key ones are summarised below:

1 Intellectual property laws e.g. patents and copyright protection.
2 Technical barriers to trade including labelling rules and stringent sanitary standards. These rules and regulations increase product compliance costs and act as a friction cost for importers.
3 Preferential state procurement policies – where government favour local producers when finalising contracts for state spending.
4 Domestic subsidies – aid for domestic businesses facing financial problems e.g. subsidies for car manufacturers or loss-making airlines.
5 Financial protectionism – e.g. when a government instructs banks to give priority when making loans to domestic businesses.
6 Murky or hidden protectionism - e.g. state measures that indirectly discriminate against foreign workers, investors and traders.
7 Managed exchange rates – government intervention in currency markets to affect relative prices of imports and exports.

Example of non-tariff barrier

Until recently China ruled that all avocados coming from countries such as Kenya had to be frozen to -30°C and peeled before shipping

Main arguments against protectionism

The **conventional view** is that import tariffs nearly always lead to a deadweight loss of economic welfare mainly through the effects of higher prices for consumers and also the distorting effects of a tariff on market competition, prices and the allocation of scarce resources.

- Risk of retaliation and a possible trade war
- Market distortions
- Higher prices for consumers
- Regressive effect on income inequality
- Incentives to by-pass controls in shadow markets
- Higher costs for exporters

Main drawbacks:

1 **Resource misallocation** leading to a loss of economic efficiency
2 **Dangers of retaliation** and risks of a persistent trade war as countries engage in tit for tat responses
3 **Potential for more corruption** because tariffs are higher in less democratic countries, and revenues can be appropriated

4. **Higher prices for domestic consumers** which has a regressive impact on poorer people / communities
5. **Increased input costs for home producers** which damages competitiveness for businesses that require key imported component parts and raw materials that are subject to an import tariff or stringent quota
6. **Barrier to entry** because protectionism reduces market contestability and thereby increases monopoly power

When evaluating the impact of a protectionist policy it is always a good idea to consider the possible effects on **different stakeholders** – these might include:
- Domestic producers
- Consumers
- Foreign producers
- The government

Example: Tariff analysis – using concepts of consumer and producer surplus:

Import tariffs tend to be good for domestic producers and the government but bad news for domestic consumers of a product to which a tariff is applied. Tariffs increase the price for domestic consumers – this leads to a contraction in demand and leads to lower consumer surplus.

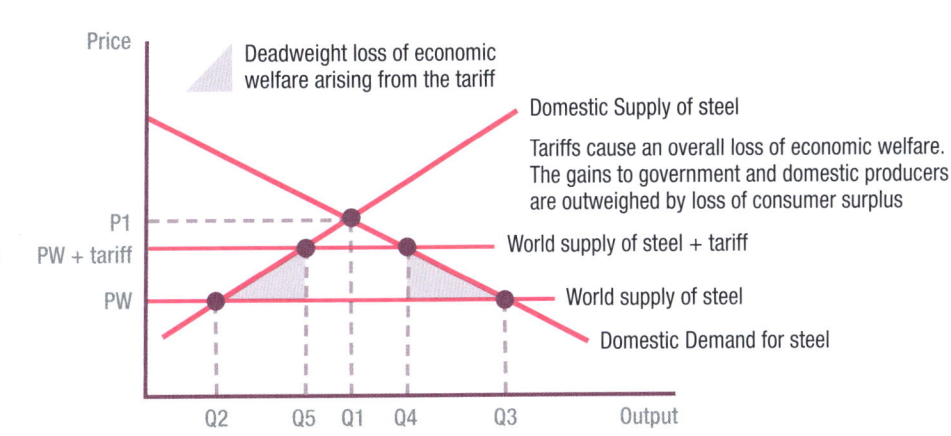

Import tariffs increase the market price and therefore increase domestic producer revenue – a gain in producer surplus

Deadweight loss of economic welfare arising from the tariff

Tariffs cause an overall loss of economic welfare. The gains to government and domestic producers are outweighed by loss of consumer surplus

(Graph: Price vs Output showing Domestic Supply of steel, Domestic Demand for steel, World supply of steel (PW), World supply of steel + tariff (PW + tariff), with P1 at domestic equilibrium, and quantities Q2, Q5, Q1, Q4, Q3)

	Impact	Evaluation
Domestic producers	Producers benefit initially from an import tariff – they are protected from lower priced imports and can expect an increase in output at a higher price which increases their revenues and operating profits.	Possible X-inefficiencies because of reduction in intensity of market competition. Other producers affected e.g. a tariff on steel raises the cost of car and construction companies.
Foreign (overseas) producers	Import tariff is a barrier to trade and squeezes demand leading to lower revenues and profits.	Producers may be able to shift production / exports to countries or regions where import tariffs are lower.
Consumers	Consumers face higher prices after the tariff – leading to a fall in real incomes. May affect lower income households more – regressive? Loss of consumer choice (lower utility).	Impact on demand depends on the price elasticity of demand for the affected product. Tariffs on essential items such as foodstuffs tend to have a lower price elasticity of demand.
The government	Government tax revenues rise initially from having import tariffs – rising GDP and increasing profitability of suppliers.	Adverse effects of possible retaliatory tariffs on other industries. Slower economic growth from higher inflation.

> **Exam Tip** Each country must consider the strength of the arguments for and against trade restrictions – often on a case-by-case basis. A lot might depend for example on the economic circumstances prevailing at a particular time and also their longer-term trade and development strategy.

4.1.7 BALANCE OF PAYMENTS

What you need to know

Components of the balance of payments:
- The current account
- The capital and financial accounts

Causes of deficits and surpluses on the current account

Measures to reduce a country's imbalance on the current account

Significance of global trade imbalances

Current account

The current account of a nation's balance of payments is made up of **four separate balances**:
1. Net balance of **trade in goods**
2. Net balance of **trade in services**
3. **Net primary income** (includes interest, profits, dividends)
4. **Net secondary income** (includes transfers i.e. contributions to EU, military aid, overseas aid and migrant remittances)

Trade Balance in Goods (X-M)
- Manufactured goods, components, raw materials
- Energy products, capital technology

Trade Balance in Services (X-M)
- Banking, Insurance, Consultancy
- Tourism, Transport, Logistics
- Shipping, Education, Health,
- Research, Arts

Net Primary Income from Overseas Assets
- Profits, interest and dividends from investments in other countries
- Net remittance flows from migrant workers living and working overseas

Net Secondary Income
- Overseas aid / debt relief transfers
- Military grants
- UK Payments to the European Union (prior to the UK's Brexit)

> **COMMON ERROR ALERT!**
> It is important not to confuse the terms 'current account balance' and 'trade balance' – the trade balance forms part of the current account, but is not absolutely identical! If you are faced with questions about causes of current account deficits and surpluses, remember that this is a different question from one about causes of trade deficits and surpluses, so you should ensure that you mention net primary income and net secondary income as well.

Capital account

The capital account of the balance of payments is a small element of it. The main items included are the following:
- Sale/transfer of patents, copyrights, franchises, leases and other transferable contracts (example would be international buying and selling of land by businesses)
- Debt forgiveness/cancellation (forgiving debt is counted as a negative in this account)
- Capital transfers of ownership of fixed assets (i.e. international death duties)

Financial account

The financial account includes transactions that result in a change of ownership of financial assets and liabilities between UK residents and non-residents – this includes:

1. Net balance of foreign direct investment flows (FDI)
2. Net balance of portfolio investment flows (e.g. inflows/outflows of debt and equity)
3. Balance of banking flows (e.g. hot money flowing in/out of banking system)
4. Changes to the value of reserves of gold and foreign currency

What is foreign direct investment?

FDI is investment from one country into another (normally by companies rather than governments) that involves establishing operations or acquiring tangible assets, including stakes in other businesses.

Foreign direct investment flows:
- Inward investment is a positive for the UK accounts
  - E.g. an overseas business decides to build a manufacturing factory in the UK
  - A foreign retail firm invests to open new stores in the UK
- Outward investment is a negative for the UK financial account of the balance of payments
  - Investment made overseas by UK businesses

What are portfolio investment flows?

Portfolio investment happens when people / businesses from one country buy shares or other securities such as bonds in other nations.
- For example:
  - A UK investor buys some shares in Google (this is a portfolio investment outflow for the UK accounts)
  - A German investment bank might buy some of the sovereign debt issued by the UK government (this counts as a portfolio investment inflow for the UK)

Causes of deficits on the current account

If a nation is running a **current account deficit**, this is known as an external deficit
- It involves a **net outflow of income** from the economy's circular flow
- Deficit countries need to run a **financial account surplus** to achieve balance on their external accounts
- This might be achieved for example by attracting inflows of financial capital (e.g. FDI) from **other countries**
- Current account deficit nations are **debtor countries**

> **Exam Tip** It is important to understand that there are **short term, medium-term and long-term causes** of a current account deficit. And also, that not all of the causes of a deficit are necessarily the result of a poorly-performing economy. It is a good idea to make a distinction between **cyclical and structural causes** of a deficit.

Key causes of a current account deficit

- Poor price and non-price competitiveness which is perhaps the result of:
  - Higher inflation than trading partners over a lengthy period of time
  - Low levels of capital investment and research and development spending
  - Weaknesses in design, branding and product performance affecting non-price competitiveness
- Strong exchange rate affecting demand for exports and imports
  - A high currency value increases the overseas prices of exports leading to a fall in demand
  - Appreciating currency also makes imports cheaper leading to rising import demand from consumers
- Recession in one or more major trade partner countries
  - Recession cuts value of exports to these countries

Continues on next page

- Volatile global prices (e.g. soft and hard commodities)
  - Exporters of primary commodities might be hit by a fall in global prices and therefore a direct fall in the value of their export earnings
  - Importing nations could be hit by higher world prices for oil and gas, raw materials
  - If demand for imports is price inelastic, then increased world prices will cause higher spending on imports
- Strong domestic economic growth can also be a cause of a widening current account deficit
- Rising demand for imported raw materials and component parts used by domestic industries

Structural causes of a current account deficit include:
1. Relatively low productivity / high unit labour costs
2. Insufficient investment in capital which limits a nation's export capacity
3. Low levels of national saving
4. Long term declines in the real prices of a country's major exports

Consequences from a current account deficit
1. A loss of aggregate demand if there is a trade deficit (M>X) causes weaker real GDP growth and might lead to reduced living standards and rising unemployment
2. Big current account deficits will usually cause the currency to depreciate, leading to higher cost-push inflation and a deterioration in the terms of trade
3. Some countries running current account deficits may choose to borrow to achieve a financial account surplus but this increase in external debt carries risks especially if interest rates rise
4. Unsustainable current account deficits can ultimately lead to a loss of investor confidence, leading to capital flight and a possible currency / balance of payments crisis

Causes of a current account surplus

What is a current account surplus?
A current account surplus means that there is a net injection of income into a country's circular flow. Surplus nations are also known as **creditor countries** and – other things being the same – a surplus will lead to an accumulation of foreign exchange e.g. from rising export sales or an increase in net primary and secondary income.

What are the main causes of a current account surplus?
A large, persistent current account surplus results from:
- A large and persistent surplus of savings (S) over investment (I) for households, firms and the government. In these countries, consumption could be higher, and this would help to rebalance trade
- A large positive gap between exports and imports, when net income balance and net transfers are small
- High world prices for exports of commodities such as oil and gas.

A surplus on the current account would allow a deficit to be run on the financial account.
- For example, surplus foreign currency can be used to fund investment in assets located overseas
- For example, some current account surplus countries have large sovereign wealth funds
- Current account surplus countries nearly always have a strong exchange rate as a result

> **Exam Tip** A surplus is not necessarily the result of a country achieving a high level of price and non-price competitiveness. It could simply be that a country is benefitting from strong world demand for and prices of their major exports.

Measures to reduce a country's imbalance on the current account
- **Expenditure switching policies**
  - These are policies designed to change the relative prices of exports and imports
  - For example an exchange rate devaluation ought to improve the price competitiveness of exports and also make imports more expensive when priced in a domestic currency
  - Import tariffs are also designed to create expenditure-switching effects

- **Expenditure reducing policies**
    - These are policies designed to lower real incomes and AD and thereby cut demand for imports
    - E.g. higher direct taxes, cuts in government spending or an increase in monetary policy interest rates

> **Exam Tip** When asked to analyse and evaluate policies for example to reduce a current account deficit, it is a good idea to make a distinction between **expenditure-switching measures** and **expenditure-reducing policies**. It is also really important to match the policy to the cause!

Expenditure Switching Policy	Effect of Policy	Evaluative Comment
Devaluation of the exchange rate	Reduces relative price of exports and makes imports more expensive	Risk of cost-push inflation – which erodes competitive boost and fall in real incomes
Import tariffs	Increases the price of imports and makes domestic output more price competitive	Risk of retaliation from other countries if import tariffs are used as BoP policy
Low rate of inflation (perhaps deflation)	Keeps general price level under control and makes exports more competitive	Risks from deflation as a way of achieving internal devaluation – including lower investment

Expenditure Reducing Policy	Effect of Policy	Evaluative Comment
Increase in income taxes	Reduces real disposable incomes causing falling demand for imports	Cut in living standards and risk of damage to work incentives in labour market
Cuts in real level of government spending	Lowers aggregate demand, firms may look to export their spare capacity	Damage to short term economic growth, risks that austerity hits investment
Low rate of inflation (perhaps deflation)	Keeps general price level under control and makes exports more competitive	Risks from deflation as a way of achieving internal devaluation – including lower investment

Governments may also decide to use **supply-side policies**. These can increase output and reduce the domestic price level (which makes exports more price competitive). Supply side policies can also lead to innovation, making exports more desirable.

Changes in the exchange rate and adjustment of a current account deficit

To what extent is a current account deficit corrected by changes in a country's exchange rate? In theory, a large current account deficit leads to an outflow of currency from the circular flow which then causes an exchange rate depreciation (within a floating currency system). And a weaker currency in theory helps bring about an adjustment of the trade balance as exports become more competitive in overseas markets and imported goods and services appear more expensive in domestic markets. In reality, the extent to which a current depreciation helps to improve the trade balance depends on a number of factors and you need to understand the J curve effect and the associated Marshall-Lerner condition.

The J curve effect

In the short term, a currency depreciation may not improve the current account of the Balance of Payments. This is because the price elasticities of demand for exports and imports are likely to be inelastic in the short term. Initially the quantity of imports bought will remain steady in part because contracts for imported goods are already signed. Export demand will be inelastic in response to the exchange rate change as it takes time for export businesses to increase their sales following a fall in prices. Earnings from selling more exports may be insufficient to compensate for higher total spending on imports. The balance of trade may therefore initially worsen. This is known as the 'J curve' effect.

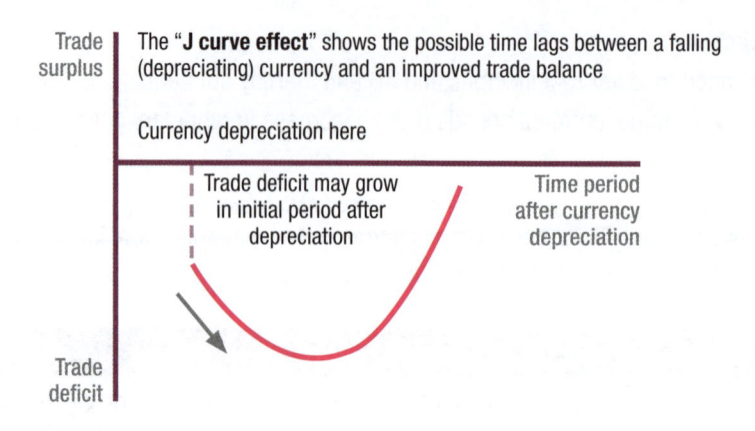

Trade surplus

The "**J curve effect**" shows the possible time lags between a falling (depreciating) currency and an improved trade balance

Currency depreciation here

Trade deficit may grow in initial period after depreciation

Time period after currency depreciation

Trade deficit

The Marshall Lerner Condition

Marshall Lerner condition states that a depreciation / devaluation of the exchange rate will lead to a net improvement in the trade balance provided that the **sum of the price elasticity of demand for exports and imports > 1** (it is easiest to ignore the minus sign for PED in this instance).

	PED for exports	PED for imports	Sum of price elasticity of demand for X and M	Will fall in currency improve the trade balance?
Country A	0.4	0.3	0.7	No
Country B	1.2	0.7	1.9	Yes
Country C	0.8	0.2	1.0	Will leave it unchanged

> **Exam Tip** The J-curve effect and the Marshall-Lerner condition are effective ways to evaluate the impact of exchange rate changes. However, the best students will always try to put these evaluative points in context. For example, they might consider the goods/services typically traded by a particular country (e.g. the UK exports financial services & tourism, and imports food / energy / raw materials) and make a judgement about the likelihood of the Marshall-Lerner or J-curve effects occurring.

Significance of global trade imbalances

What are global trade imbalances?
Imbalances refer to persistent current account **surpluses** for some countries contrasted with **deficits** in other nations.

Theory suggests that in a freely-floating exchange rate system, trade imbalances will self-correct. This is because if, say, a country has a trade deficit, then demand for exports will be low which in turn causes reduced demand for the currency. This leads to a depreciation of the currency, thus making exports more price competitive and stimulating demand for them. However, imbalances often tend to persist, because a) not every country operates a freely-floating exchange rate and b) there may be structural reasons why some countries run persistent trade deficits or surpluses.

Why do they matter?
The balance of payments will balance overall. That is to say, a deficit on the current account must be matched by surpluses on the capital/financial accounts (in reality, it is very difficult to carry out accurate accounting and so there is always a 'net errors and omissions' term which allows the BoP to balance). For there to be a persistent deficit on the current account, there must be a corresponding persistent surplus on the financial account – the economy must be able to attract inflows of capital (either long-term capital such as FDI…which is desirable…or short-term capital in the form of hot money…which is less desirable)

- Deficit countries:
  - Run up large external debts and are reliant on foreign capital
  - May decide to switch towards using protectionist policies
  - Deficits can lead to a fall in relative living standards over time if economic growth slows down

- Surplus countries:
  - Are saving more than they spend, thereby depressing global economic demand and growth
  - May be adopting a policy to keep their currency deliberately under-valued
  - Might be under-consuming (thus affecting living standards) and allocating domestic scarce resources to exporting overseas rather than allowing higher levels of domestic consumer spending

> **Exam Tip** One of the major issues with trade imbalances is that they strengthen the arguments of those who want to move away from free trade in goods and services. Significant trade imbalances have been a factor behind the rise of **de-globalisation** in recent years – i.e. they **create trade tensions** that can lead to widespread use of **tariff and non-tariff barriers**.

4.1.8 EXCHANGE RATES

What you need to know

Exchange rate systems: floating, fixed, managed

Meaning of revaluation/appreciation and devaluation/depreciation

Factors influencing floating exchange rates

Government intervention in currency markets through foreign currency transactions and the use of interest rates

Competitive devaluation/depreciation and its consequences

Impact of changes in exchange rates on macroeconomic objectives and FDI flows

What is an exchange rate?

An exchange rate is the rate at which one country's currency can be exchanged for other currencies in the foreign exchange (FX) market. There is no such thing as "the" exchange rate – so if £ depreciates against the $, it could still be appreciating against the Euro or the Japanese Yen.

Effective exchange rate: This is a weighted index of sterling's value against a basket of currencies in which the weights are based on the importance of trade between the UK and each country.

What are the main exchange rate systems?

- **A free-floating currency** where the external value of a currency depends wholly on market forces of supply and demand – there is no central bank intervention
- **A managed-floating currency** when the central bank may choose to intervene in the foreign exchange markets to affect the value of a currency to meet specific macroeconomic objectives
- **A fixed exchange rate system** e.g. a hard currency peg either as part of a currency board system or membership of the ERM Mark II for those EU countries eventually intending to join the Euro

Describing changes in exchange rates carefully and accurately

You should be aware that a depreciation and devaluation are different, even if they ultimately have the same consequences:

- **Depreciation** is a fall in the value of a currency in a floating exchange rate system
- **Devaluation** is a fall in the value of a currency in a fixed exchange rate system
- **Appreciation** is a rise in the value of a currency in a floating exchange rate system
- **Revaluation** is a rise in the value of a currency in a fixed exchange rate system

Choice of currency system for selected countries

	US Dollar ($)	Euro	Composite Currency or Other Currency Peg
Fixed currency with no separate legal tender	Ecuador, Zimbabwe	Kosovo, San Marino	
Currency board system	Hong Kong	Bulgaria	
Conventional exchange rate peg (fixed currency system)	Qatar, Saudi Arabia	Denmark, Senegal	Kuwait, Nepal
Crawling exchange rate peg (semi-fixed currency)	Jamaica	Croatia	China
Managed floating currency	Kenya, Brazil, Ukraine, South Korea, India, Zambia, South Africa, Thailand, Turkey, Sweden, Mexico, Israel, Japan, Chile		
Free floating exchange rate	Australia, Canada, Norway, UK, USA, Euro Zone, Ethiopia		

Free floating exchange rates

In a free-floating currency system (an example being the £ sterling against all other currencies):
- The external value of the currency is set by market forces
    - The strength of currency supply and demand drives the external value of a currency in the markets
    - The currency can either appreciate (rise) or depreciate (fall)
- There is no intervention by the central bank
    - Central bank allows the currency to find its own market level
    - It does not alter interest rates or intervene directly by buying/selling currencies to influence the price
- There is no target for the exchange rate
    - External value of currency is not an intermediate target of monetary policy (i.e. interest rates not set to influence the currency)

What factors cause changes in the currency in a floating system?

1 **Trade balances** – countries that have strong trade and current account surpluses tend (other factors remaining the same) to see their currencies appreciate as money flows into the circular flow from exports of goods and services and from investment income
   - A good 'rule of thumb' is that demand for exports tends to affect the demand for currency curve (because if people overseas want to buy UK exports they will need to buy £s in order to pay for them), whereas demand for imports tends to affect the supply of currency (because we need to supply £s to the foreign exchange market to buy foreign currencies to pay for imports)
2 **Foreign direct investment (FDI)** – an economy that attracts high net inflows of capital investment (i.e. long-term capital flows) from overseas will see an increase in currency demand and a rising exchange rate
3 **Portfolio investment** – strong inflows of portfolio investment into equities and bonds from overseas can cause a currency to appreciate
4 **Interest rate differentials** - countries with relatively high interest rates can expect to see '**hot money**' (i.e. short-term capital) flows coming in and causing an appreciation of the exchange rate
5 **Speculation** – this is responsible for much of the day-to-day volatility

Market diagrams to represent the Foreign Exchange Market look just like regular market diagrams, just with slight changes to the axes labels e.g. quantity of currency on the x-axis and value of the currency in terms of another on the y-axis.

Chain of reasoning – the impact of higher interest rates on a floating exchange rate:

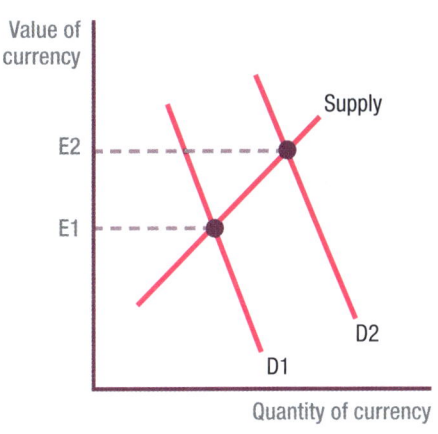

Rise in policy interest rates by central bank
↓
Currency more attractive for investors
↓
Attracts inflows of short term hot money
↓
Causes outward shift in currency demand
↓
Currency appreciates in value in a floating system

Chain of reasoning – the effect of a fall in export demand on a floating exchange rate:

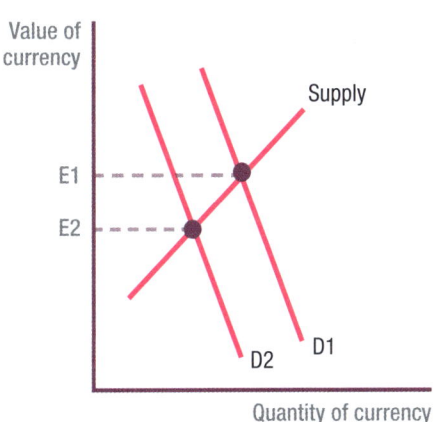

Recession in a trading partner
↓
Causes a fall in export sales
↓
Worsening of trade balance
↓
Inward shift of currency demand
↓
Currency will depreciate

Managed floating exchange rates

With **managed exchange rates**:
- Currency is usually set by market forces
    - Central bank gives a degree of freedom for market exchange rates on a daily basis
- A central bank may **intervene** occasionally to influence the price:
    - Buying to support a currency (i.e. selling their foreign exchange reserves)
    - Selling to weaken a currency (i.e. adding to their foreign exchange reserves)
    - Changes in policy interest rates to affect hot money flows i.e. increase rates to attract inflows of money into the banking system looking for a favourable rate of return
- In a managed floating system, the currency becomes a key target of monetary policy
    - Higher exchange rate might be wanted to control demand-pull and cost-push inflationary pressures
    - A government might want to engineer a competitive devaluation to improve export competitiveness

Policy tools for managing floating exchange rates
- Changes in monetary policy interest rates
    - Changes in interest rates e.g. lower interest rates to depreciate the exchange rate
    - Causes movements of "hot money" banking flows into or out of a country
- Quantitative easing
    - Increase liquidity in the banking system leading to lower interest rates, usually causes outflow of money and a depreciation of the exchange rate
- Direct buying / selling in the currency market (intervention)
    - Direct intervention in the currency market
    - Buying and selling of domestic / foreign currencies
- Taxation of overseas currency deposits and capital controls
    - Taxation of foreign deposits in banks cut the profit from hot money inflows
    - Controls on the free flow of capital into and out of a country

Chain of reasoning: how can a central bank influence the value of a currency?

In a **managed floating currency system**, one way that a central bank can influence the external value is by changing interest rates.

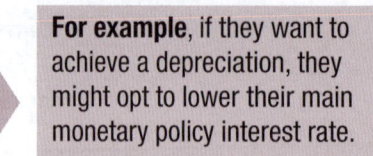

For example, if they want to achieve a depreciation, they might opt to lower their main monetary policy interest rate.

A fall in interest rates reduces the returns on overseas money held in a country's banking system. The real return may become negative.

As a result, lower interest rates might cause an outflow of short-term "hot money" from commercial banks to other countries.

This will cause an outward shift of the supply curve for the currency as investors look for currencies with higher expected returns.

In this way, assuming other central banks have kept their rates constant, a fall in interest rates might lead to a depreciation.

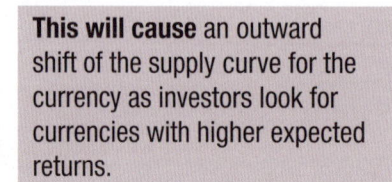

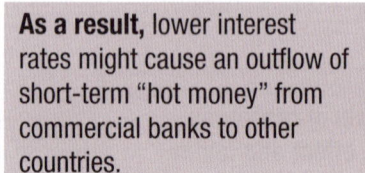

Competitive devaluations / dirty floating
- Competitive devaluations occur when a country deliberately intervenes to drive down the value of their currency to provide a competitive lift to demand, output and jobs in their export industries
- They may try this when faced with a deflationary recession or perhaps to attract extra foreign investment
- For nations with persistent trade deficits and rising unemployment, a competitive devaluation of the exchange rate can become an attractive option - but there are also risks involved
- Devaluing an exchange rate can be seen by other countries as a form of trade protectionism that invites some form of retaliatory action such as an import tariff
- Cutting the exchange rate makes it harder for other countries to export negatively affecting their growth rate which in turn can damage the volume of trade that takes place between nations
- Competitive devaluations of a currency go against the principles of trade based on comparative advantage

Fixed exchange rates
In a fixed exchange rate system:
- The government / central bank fixes the currency value
    - External value is pegged to one or more currencies (known as the anchor currency)
    - The central bank must hold sufficient foreign exchange reserves in order to intervene in currency markets to maintain the fixed peg
        - i.e. they may need to buy domestic currency using foreign currency to push up the value of their domestic currency
        - Holding foreign exchange reserves can create an opportunity cost
- Pegged exchange rate becomes official rate
    - Trade takes place at this official exchange rate
    - There might be unofficial trades in shadow currency markets
- Adjustable peg
    - Occasional realignments may be needed
    - E.g. a devaluation or revaluation depending on economic circumstances – the currency may have drifted from the fundamental value

Impacts of changes in exchange rates
What happens when the exchange rate changes?
As an exchange rate changes, so does the value of amounts converted using the new exchange rate. Here is an example:

Amount	Exchange Rate	Conversion
€100,000	£1 = €1.25	£80,000
€100,000	£1 = €1.10	£90,909
€100,000	£1 = €1.50	£66,666

Ways exchange rates impact business activity
1. Price of exports in international markets
2. Cost of goods bought from overseas
3. Revenues and profits earned overseas
4. Converting cash receipts from customers overseas

Example: Who benefits or loses from a lower exchange rate?

Winners	Losers
Businesses exporting into international markets	Businesses importing goods and services
Businesses earning substantial profits in overseas currencies	Overseas businesses trying to compete in the domestic market

To remember the opposite (higher exchange rate)
SPICEE: Strong Pound Imports Cheaper Exports Expensive – this is a frequently used mnemonic!

Impact of a currency depreciation
- A currency depreciation usually has a similar effect on the macro-economy as a cut in interest rates
- A currency depreciation may help to provide a partial auto-correction of a large trade deficit.

Macro objective	Comment on the impact of a currency depreciation
Inflation	Higher import prices feed into increased consumer prices which may help a country to avoid deflation and it also lowers real interest rates. But higher inflation threatens real living standards especially for groups with weak bargaining power in the labour market who are unable to bid for higher wages.
Economic growth	A weaker currency is usually a stimulus to GDP growth e.g. from higher net exports but much depends on the price elasticity of demand for exports and imports. Also, many exports require imported components which will have become more expensive as a result of the depreciation.
Unemployment	A more competitive currency will help to increase domestic production and perhaps create a positive export multiplier effect which will further stimulate aggregate demand and jobs. There might also be an upturn in tourism / demand from overseas students to come to a country's universities.
Balance of trade	Dependent on price elasticities of demand for X&M – possible J curve effect in the short run. The impact on export sales also depends in part on the strength of GDP growth in key export markets.
Business investment	Should help to improve profitability e.g. a fall in the external value of the £ increases the overseas earnings of UK plc in US dollars and Euros which will be now be worth more in £s.
Wider effects	Depreciation is similar to a cut in interest rates (i.e. expansionary monetary policy) but there are risks too – including higher costs of importing components, raw materials and prices of important capital technologies.
FDI	Depreciation of a currency makes a country's FDI assets (i.e. investments abroad that are denominated in foreign currency) appear more valuable when converted into the domestic currency. Likewise, FDI liabilities (i.e. investments in the domestic economy from overseas, denominated in the domestic currency) appear less valuable to overseas investors. This can ultimately therefore reduce inwards FDI.

Exam Tip When discussing the impact of exchange rate changes, remember to use **aggregate demand and supply analysis** from **Theme 2** to help support your arguments. E.g. you might show an outward shift in AD (rising exports) and an inward shift of AS (higher import costs) resulting from a significant depreciation in the external value of the exchange rate.

Chain of reasoning: how might a currency depreciation affect international competitiveness?

| A depreciation is a fall in the external value of a currency inside a floating exchange rate system. | ▶ | Consider for example, a depreciation of the UK £ (sterling) against the Euro. The £ might fall from Euro 1.50 to Euro 1.20, a drop of 20%. | ▶ | **As a result**, the foreign price of goods and services sold overseas falls. |

| A rise in import prices will make domestic producers in the UK appear relatively more competitive purely in cost and price terms. | ◀ | In addition, the UK price of imported products will increase because £1 buys fewer euros. For example, imported cars will be more expensive. | ◀ | **This makes** UK exports relatively cheaper in overseas markets. Relative export prices fall leading to improved competitiveness. |

Evaluating effects of a currency depreciation

In theory, a depreciation of the exchange rate stimulates aggregate demand but this depends on:

1. The variable length of time lags as consumers and businesses respond
2. The scale of any change in the exchange rate i.e. 5%, 10%, 20%
3. Whether the change in a currency is temporary or longer-lasting
4. The coefficients of price elasticity of demand for X&M (relate this back to the Marshall-Lerner condition)
5. The size of any second-round multiplier and accelerator effects
6. When the currency movement takes place – i.e. which stage of an economic cycle (recession, recovery etc.)
7. The type of economy (e.g. the impact will be different for small developing nations v large advanced countries)
8. The degree of openness of the economy to international trade i.e. measured by the value of trade as a % of GDP

Evaluating exchange rate systems

Evaluating floating exchange rates

- Advantages of floating exchange rates
  - Reduces the need for a central bank to hold large amounts of currency reserves
  - Freedom to set monetary policy interest rates to meet domestic objectives
  - May help to prevent imported inflation
  - Insulation for an economy after an external shock especially for export-dependent countries
  - Partial automatic correction for a current account deficit
  - Less risk of a currency becoming significantly over/undervalued
- Evaluation
  - No guarantee that floating exchange rates will be stable
  - Volatility in a floating currency might be detrimental to attracting inward investment
  - A lower (more competitive) exchange rate does not necessarily correct a persistent balance of payments deficit - consider the J curve theory and also the importance of non-price competitiveness

Using AD-AS analysis

Consider the likely impact of an **exchange rate appreciation**:

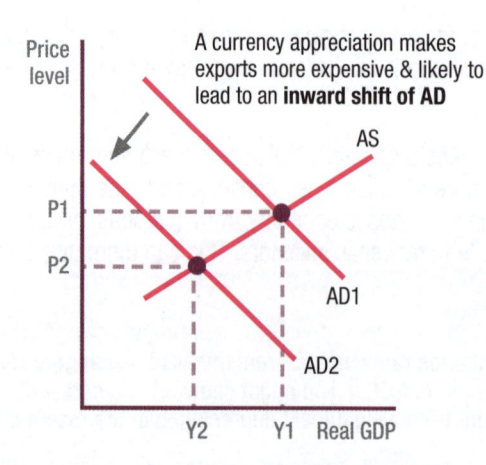

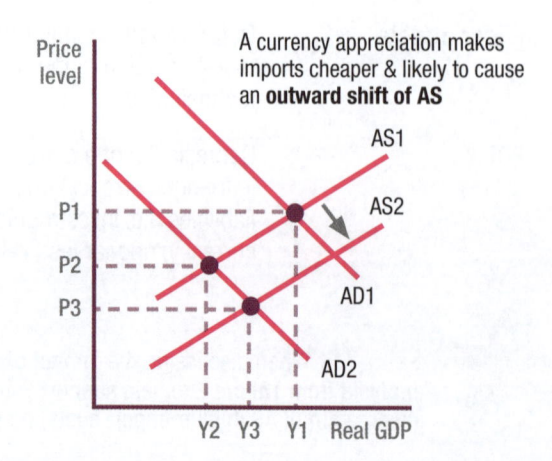

A currency appreciation makes exports more expensive & likely to lead to an **inward shift of AD**

A currency appreciation makes imports cheaper & likely to cause an **outward shift of AS**

Evaluating fixed exchange rates

- Advantages of fixed exchange rates
  - Certainty of currency value gives confidence for inward investment from overseas businesses
  - Reduced costs of "currency hedging" for businesses such as airlines
  - Currency stability helps to control inflation i.e. it is a discipline on businesses to keep labour costs low
  - A stable currency can lead to lower borrowing costs i.e. lower yields on government bonds
  - Imposes responsibility on government macro policies e.g. to keep inflation under control
  - Less speculation in the currency market if the fixed exchange rate is regarded by traders as credible
- Evaluation
  - Reduced freedom to use interest rates for other macro objectives such as stimulating GDP growth
  - Many developing countries do not have sufficient foreign currency reserves to maintain a fixed exchange rate
  - Difficult for countries to use a competitive devaluation of their fixed exchange rate – this creates political tensions and might lead to a protectionist response
  - Devaluation of a fixed exchange rate can lead to a surge in cost-push inflation – this is damaging for competitiveness and has regressive effects on poorer families

Floating versus fixed exchange rates

- Fixed rates may be optimal for developing countries wanting to control inflation
- Export-dependent economies may favour a managed floating rate e.g. to offset fluctuating world prices
- Not every country has the reserves to influence currency
- Choice of currency regime is hugely important for developing countries
- Some countries have opted to join a monetary union e.g. the nineteen members of the Euro Zone

4.1.9 INTERNATIONAL COMPETITIVENESS

What you need to know

Measures of international competitiveness: relative unit labour costs and relative export prices

Factors influencing international competitiveness

Significance of international competitiveness
- Benefits of being internationally competitive
- Problems of being internationally uncompetitive

What is competitiveness?
External competitiveness is the sustained ability to sell goods and services profitably at competitive prices overseas.

What is the difference between price and non-price competitiveness?

Price (or cost) competitiveness
- Key measure: differences in relative unit labour cost

Non-price competitiveness
- Key aspects: product quality, innovation, design, reliability and performance, choice, after-sales services, marketing, branding, brand loyalty and the availability and cost of replacement parts

Non-wage cost factors include
1. Environmental taxes e.g. minimum prices on carbon emissions
2. Employment protection laws and health and safety regulations
3. Statutory requirements for employer pensions
4. Employment taxes e.g. employers' national insurance costs

> **Exam Tip** You need be aware that competitiveness can relate to **price and non-price factors**. Also, that a range of demand and supply-side policies might be needed in order for competitiveness to be improved over time.

Relative unit labour costs

Unit labour costs are labour costs per unit of output. There is a simple formula for calculating unit labour costs:

Unit labour costs = total labour costs / total output

Unit labour costs are determined mainly by:

1. Average wages / salaries in a country's labour market – one measure tracked is the hourly labour cost of employing people in the labour market
2. Labour productivity i.e. output per person employed or output per hour worked

Key analysis point: unit labour costs will tend to rise when wages are rising faster than productivity

How to lower relative unit labour costs

- Relative unit labour costs will rise when
  - A country's exchange rate appreciates
  - Wage costs rise relatively faster than other nations
  - Labour productivity growth is relatively slower
- Options for reducing relative unit labour costs
  - Monetary policy interventions aimed at a currency depreciation e.g. a managed floating exchange rate
  - Wage controls e.g. wage/pay freezes in the public sector
  - Supply-side measures designed to raise labour productivity / efficiency across many industries

Relative export prices

Relative export prices are one country's export prices in relation to other countries, usually expressed as an index.

Relative export prices will rise when:

1. There is an appreciation of the currency – causing export prices in overseas markets to rise
2. There is a period of high relative inflation in one country compared to others – again this tends to make exports appear more expensive when priced in an overseas currency
3. When export businesses experience higher costs e.g. arising from environmental taxes or increased minimum wages, which leads them to raise price to protect their profit margins
4. When exporters of goods and services are hit by import tariffs

Competitiveness rankings

The annual Global Competitiveness Index published by the World Economic Forum (WEF) uses a range of indicators:

Indicator	Brief comment on the indicator
Effectiveness of institutions	Protection of property rights, rule of law, corruption
Quality of infrastructure	Quality of transport, communications, energy etc.
Macroeconomic performance	Inflation, fiscal balance, government debt, growth
Health and primary education	Malaria incidence, prevalence of HIV, mortality rates
Higher education and training	Quality of teaching and attainment e.g. in maths
Efficiency of goods & labour markets	Intensity of competition, tariffs, other barriers
Technological readiness	Internet use, availability of latest technologies
Sophistication of business	Supplier quality, business clusters
Innovation	Patent applications, research & development spend

Policies to improve competitiveness

These policies might include:
1. Competitive exchange rate – perhaps involving a managed floating currency
2. Competitive tax environment to attract inward investment and encourage new business start-ups
3. Investment in human capital to improve the quality of the workforce
4. Increased research & development to drive a faster pace of innovation
5. Stronger market competition to raise factor productivity and lower relative export prices
6. Stable macroeconomic environment e.g. maintaining low inflation with steady economic growth to support business confidence
7. Investment in critical infrastructure such as better road, air and rail links, improved ports, faster broadband and fibre-optic internet connections

Competitiveness is strongly affected by the **pace of innovation** in different markets and industries.

| R&D tax credits (used in Australia & South Korea) | Patent Box Initiative – 10% corporation tax (a UK policy) | Public R&D and more funding for higher education | Highly skilled migrants policy e.g. skilled coders | Nurturing an entrepreneurial culture | Increasing intensity of competition within markets |

Innovation requires strong human capital, institutions and incentives.

Fiscal policy and international competitiveness

Fiscal policy can have an important part to play in driving competitiveness of countries:
1. Subsidies to lower the cost of research e.g. in pharmaceuticals, life sciences, robotics and artificial intelligence
2. Tax incentives can encourage the commercialisation of ideas e.g. ideas coming out of universities
3. Lower employment taxes to stimulate skilled migration from overseas
4. Lower capital gains taxes encourage small businesses / start-ups
5. Special economic zones (SEZ) to attract research-intensive businesses

What matters for competitiveness in the long run?

- Macro competitiveness has **micro foundations**:
  - Competitive markets and innovative businesses
  - Skills, aptitudes and attitudes within a diverse workforce
  - Expanding opportunities for female entrepreneurs /refugees
- Recognition that infrastructure and innovation are crucial: increasingly, competitiveness flows from smart urbanisation
- Competitive advantage comes from having:
  - Globally scaled businesses close to or at the technological frontier
  - A culture of innovative business start-ups / social entrepreneurs
  - A financial system that can provide appropriate and affordable credit for education, business research and funding for business expansion
- Reliance on currency depreciation / devaluation and wage cuts is not a sustainable competitiveness strategy
  - The most competitive countries have the highest minimum wages
  - There is a continuous global battle for the most talented workers
  - "Races to the bottom" e.g. in taxes and wages have a limited impact

Significance of international competitiveness

Benefits
- Improved living standards e.g. measured by real GNI per capita (PPP)
- Stronger trade performance from an increase in export sales
- Virtuous circle of economic growth
- Employment creation
- Higher government tax revenues

Problems
- Trade surpluses might invite a protectionist response
- Possible risks of demand-pull inflation
- Competitiveness might be achieved at the expense of growing inequality of income and wealth
- Higher productivity might be achieved at expense of a worsening work-life balance and increased incidence of mental health problems
- Increased competitiveness might cause a country's exchange rate to appreciate

Extension idea: internal and external devaluation

What is an internal devaluation?

Internal devaluation happens when a country seeks to improve price competitiveness through lowering their wage costs and increasing productivity and not reducing the external value of their exchange rate. Good examples in recent years have applied to Latvia (a Baltic State) and Greece, in the wake of a severe depression which followed the Global Financial Crisis. Ecuador has also implemented internal devaluation. An internal devaluation requires several years of low relative inflation i.e. a country's inflation rate lower than price increases in other countries. With Greece, this involved price deflation i.e. a negative rate of inflation. Internal devaluation can be brought about by fiscal austerity (via higher taxes and cuts in government spending) and/or a sharp rise in real interest rates – both impose deflationary pressure on output and prices. Internal devaluation is more likely to happen with a country that has a fixed exchange rate e.g. Ecuador has a fixed rate against the US dollar. Greece is inside the Single European Currency zone and cannot devalue unilaterally.

What is an external devaluation?

An external devaluation happens when a country operating with a fixed or semi-fixed exchange rate system decides to deliberately lower the external value of their currency against one or a range of other currencies. A devaluation of the currency means a domestic currency buys less of a foreign currency. One motivation is to make exports more price competitive in overseas markets and to make imports relatively more expensive than domestic supply. Linked aims might include reducing the size of a trade deficit and also to cut the real value of sovereign debt owed to international creditors. In theory, currency devaluation is a faster way of improving price competitiveness than an internal devaluation.

Evaluation: risks from an internal devaluation:

1. Severe loss of output and rising unemployment
2. Fall in nominal wages reduces living standards
3. Risks from sustained price deflation
4. Real value of debt increases
5. Danger of a country suffering a permanent loss of output (known as "hysteresis")

Evaluation: drawbacks from an external devaluation:

1. Increase in cost-push inflation from higher import prices
2. Reduces real incomes because of a rise in inflation
3. No guarantee that the trade deficit will improve (refer to the J curve concept)
4. Foreign creditors will demand higher interest rates on new issues of government & corporate debt
5. Currency uncertainty makes country less attractive to inward FDI

4.2.1 ABSOLUTE AND RELATIVE POVERTY

What you need to know

Distinction between absolute poverty and relative poverty

Measures of absolute poverty and relative poverty

Causes of changes in absolute poverty and relative poverty

What is the difference between absolute and relative poverty?
- **Absolute (extreme) poverty:**
  - When a household does not have sufficient income to sustain even a basic acceptable standard of living or meet people's basic needs
  - Absolute poverty thresholds will vary between developed and developing countries
  - World Bank has two extreme poverty lines:
    1) Percentage of population living below $2.15 (PPP)
    2) Percentage of population living below $3.65 (PPP)
  - Extreme poverty is multi-dimensional - it is about more than very low income per capita
- **Relative poverty**
  - A level of household income **considerably lower than the median level of income** within a country
  - The official UK relative poverty line is household disposable income of less than 60% of median income

> **Exam Tip** It is hugely important to make a clear distinction between **absolute and relative poverty**. It is possible for example for average incomes per capita to be rising (helping to lower absolute poverty) whilst at the same time, relative poverty could be growing if the gaps in income and wealth between rich and poorer households and communities get wider.

Absolute (extreme) poverty

According to data from the World Bank, extreme poverty is declining but perhaps not quickly enough to meet one of the sustainable development goals of lowering absolute poverty to less than 3% of the global population by 2030. The percentage of people living in extreme poverty globally fell to 9% in 2022 — down from 11% in 2013.
- In 2018, about half of the world's countries had extreme poverty rates below 3%.
- 41% of people in sub Saharan Africa live in extreme poverty.
- The World Bank also focuses on the concept of **shared prosperity** defined as when economic growth increases the incomes and consumption of people in the poorest 40% of the population

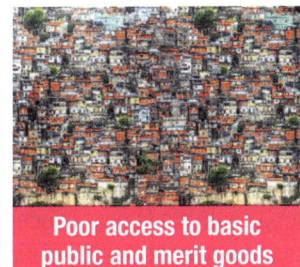

| Low and unstable household incomes | Absence of financial / welfare safety nets | Poor access to basic public and merit goods | High unemployment / low employment |

Main causes of absolute (extreme) poverty

1. Population growing faster than GDP in low income countries leading to lower per capita incomes
2. Severe savings gap – with many families unable to save and living on less than $2.15 per day
3. Absence of basic government / public services such as education and health care
4. Effects of endemic corruption in government and business
5. High levels of debt and having to pay high interest rates on loans
6. Damaging effects of civil wars and natural disasters leading to huge displacements of population
7. Low rates of formal employment, many vulnerable/insecure jobs and poverty wages
8. Absence of basic property rights which for example constrains ability to own land, claim welfare

> **Exam Tip** The causes of poverty are often **complex** and **multi-causal**. These causes will vary from country to country at different stages of economic development. Become a mini expert on a chosen cluster of developing / emerging countries and find out whether they are making significant progress in reducing extreme poverty and improving human development outcomes.

Relative Poverty

Relative poverty occurs because income and consumption are skewed across households, communities and regions. The measurement of relative poverty is covered in the next section.

Main causes of relative poverty

- Cuts in top rate income taxes in many countries increasing disposable incomes of richer households
- Surging executive pay and high rewards for skilled workers compared to other employees
- Regressive effects of higher food and energy prices on poorer households
- Deep market failures in access to good quality education, health and housing
- Declining strength of trade unions in many countries and rising monopsony power of some big employers

4.2.2 INEQUALITY

What you need to know

Distinction between income and wealth inequality
Measurements of income inequality including the Lorenz curve and Gini coefficient
Causes of income and wealth inequality within countries and between countries
Impact of economic change and development on inequality
Significance of capitalism for inequality

Income and wealth

Income is a 'flow' concept and consists of the returns that households receive as a result of providing their factors of production e.g. wages, rent, interest payments etc. Wealth is a 'stock' concept and is a measure of household assets. The distribution of income refers to how income is shared out amongst the population; clearly wealth inequality refers to how wealth is shared out amongst the population. Inequality of income and wealth are often quite closely correlated, because earning a higher income allows households to buy more assets. However, there are some exceptions e.g. some households may have low income but may have inherited wealth, and pensioners often have very low income but might be regarded as wealthy if they own their own homes or have large amounts of savings.

Measures of income inequality

- **Quintile ratio**
  - This is the ratio of the average income of the richest 20% of the population to the average income of the poorest 20% of the population
- **Gini coefficient**
  - A Gini index or coefficient of 0 represents perfect equality, while an index of 100 (or coefficient of 1) implies perfect inequality
    - This is the ratio that you really need to understand for your Edexcel economics exam

COMMON ERROR ALERT!
It is easy to get confused when interpreting the figures for the HDI and the Gini coefficient. For the HDI, a value of 0 is low development and 1 is high development. For the Gini coefficient, we need to interpret the numbers in an almost 'opposite' way i.e. 0 is high equality and 1 is total inequality.

The Lorenz Curve
The Lorenz Curve gives a visual interpretation of income or wealth inequality. It is used to plot **cumulative** share of income (or wealth) against **cumulative** share of population. The diagonal line in the graphic below shows a situation of perfect equality of income i.e. 50% of population has 50% of income. The further away from the diagonal line that the Lorenz curve lies, the greater the degree of inequality.

Using the Lorenz curve to measure the Gini coefficient

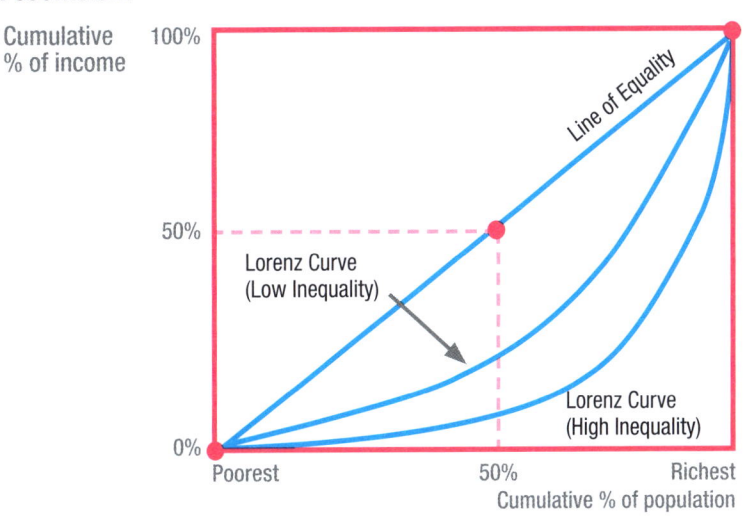

- The Gini coefficient is between 0 and 1
- A value of 0 is zero inequality and 1 is total inequality

The Gini coefficient = area A / areas A + B

Countries including South Africa, Namibia and Brazil have very high Gini coefficients. Countries such as Iceland, Slovakia and Norway have very low Gini coefficients.

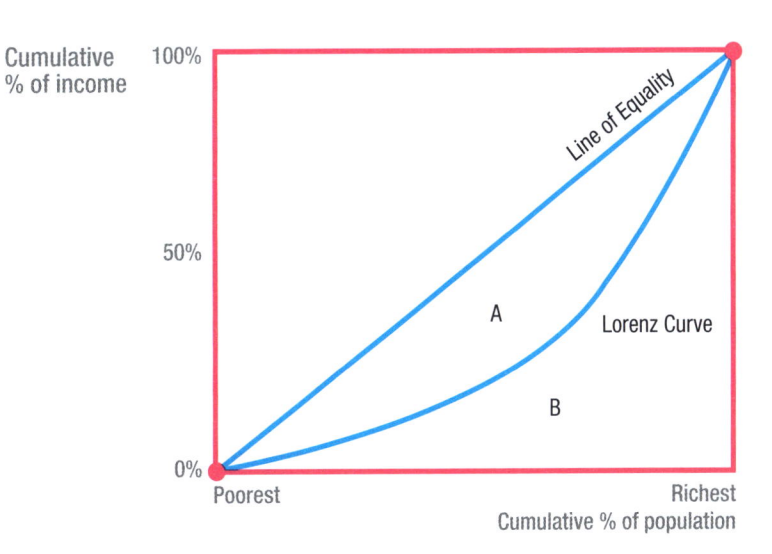

Causes of income and wealth inequality within countries and between countries

Inequalities result from the outcomes of market activity and also from the impact of inheritance and changes in taxes and benefits. Please remember that wealth can generate income and income can generate wealth.

Main causes of inequality within countries:
1. Big differences in wages and earnings in different jobs/occupations
2. Wage differentials are themselves caused by demand and supply-side factors in the labour market:
   a. Minimum educational qualifications required (a barrier to entry to certain jobs)
   b. Varying scale of trade union representation and collective bargaining power with employers
   c. Changing skill requirements of different jobs e.g. prompted by technological advances
3. The effects of unemployment especially among the long-term unemployed and younger workers
4. Damaging effects of poor health and nutrition on employment opportunities and productivity
5. Changes in the taxation of income and wealth including the extent to which a tax system is progressive on higher incomes and the wealth of the richest in a society
6. Vulnerability to loan sharks for families mired in debt – having to pay very high interest rates

Main causes of inequality between countries

The gap in per capita incomes between countries has been closing over the last two decades, in part the result of globalisation and the success that many developing / emerging nations have had in raising their economic growth rates well above population growth so that per capita incomes improve. But there remain deep-rooted inequalities in income between countries. Some of the causes are as follows:

1. Low life expectancy and fewer years of healthy life expectancy
2. Low school enrolment rates as families cannot afford education - this widens the gender opportunity gap
3. Low access to basic health care and poor nutrition which impairs brain development among the young
4. Limited access to affordable technologies – creating a digital divide
5. Much lower productivity which then leads to lower wages
6. Low real spending power limits the size of domestic markets for goods and services
7. Low prices for primary commodities – smallholder farmers have no bargaining power with transnational corporations

Impact of economic change and development on inequality

Economic changes always have an impact on the pattern of employment and the earnings available in different jobs and industries. For example, globalisation has in a number of advanced countries led to a "hollowing-out" effect meaning that there are more jobs in relatively unskilled work offering low rates of pay, fewer jobs in traditional full-time jobs in heavy industry and more jobs in high-knowledge occupations that require extensive qualifications which offer premium rates of pay.

The Kuznets Inequality Curve

The **Kuznets Curve** suggests that inequality often rises during a phase of rapid industrialisation and urbanisation but there may come a point when increased welfare provision, progressive taxes and more balanced income growth across industries might lead to a fall in overall inequality at higher per capita incomes.

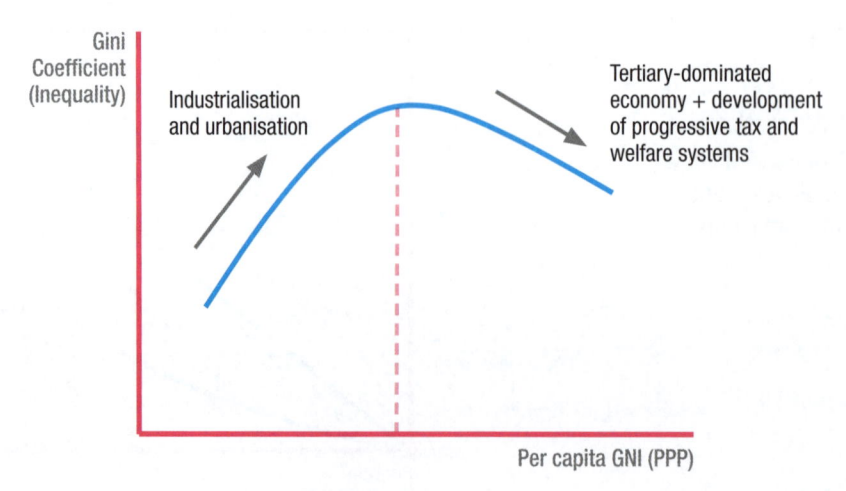

Significance of capitalism for inequality

What are the main pillars of a free market capitalist economic system?
1. Private property – people can own tangible assets such as land and financial assets such as shares
2. Self-interest – people widely assumed to act in their own rational self-interest
3. Competition in markets – assisted by the entry / exit of firms from industries
4. The price mechanism – where prices in markets act as rationing, signalling and allocation devices
5. Freedom of choice – from what to buy, which job to have, where to live
6. Limited role for government e.g. to protect private property rights, maintain currency stability

To what extent is a high income and consumption inequality an inevitable consequence of operating a capitalist system?
1. **The profit motive:** commercial businesses are assumed to be driven by the profit motive when making investment, output and employment decisions. Profits flow as dividends to shareholders and inequalities of wealth can be widened as businesses list their shares on stock markets and investors can earn capital gains as well as dividend income.
   a. However, even within a capitalist system, there are many people motivated to run their businesses as social enterprises, where profits made are reinvested for social / environmental purposes
   b. Co-operative businesses are owned by their members with profits shared out – the co-operative model has become more popular in recent years especially after the global financial crisis
   c. The government can tax high profits and incomes through a progressive tax system so that the final distribution of income in less unequal than original income
   d. Competition policy and intervention by industry regulators can help to control monopoly profits and keep real prices down for consumers
2. **A capitalist labour market:** in competitive labour markets, wages and earnings are influenced by the forces of labour demand and supply. In theory there are few limits to the pay that can be achieved by the top earners including those with very scarce skills that the market values and executives who have the power to set their own remuneration (including bonuses and share options). At the lower end of the pay scale, the majority of people earning low wages are not represented by a trade union and have little or no bargaining power with an employer.
   a. However, there are many possible interventions in labour markets that can alter the final distribution of income and help to control inequality:
      i. Minimum wage legislation setting pay floors that cannot be undercut
      ii. Legal caps on executive pay
      iii. Legal protections for employees especially in flexible jobs associated with the gig economy
   b. Government investment in human capital promoting skills and employability of vulnerable groups in society can increase earnings potential

The French economist **Thomas Piketty** wrote an influential book which argued that rising inequality was an almost inevitable consequence of capitalism. The focus of Piketty's work was the long-run evolution of the ratio of capital to income. He claimed that this will rise even further as the 21st century unfolds. Wealth will become more concentrated and inequality will rise. Piketty shows that there has been a sharp rise in the ratio of wealth to income in the early 21st century, to around 5 or 6 compared to just 2 to 3 in the 1950s and 1960s.

However, critics of Piketty counter that – over many decades - capitalism has helped make the world a more equal place. They point to the impact of globalisation driven by increasing specialisation, trade and the diffusion of new technologies as helping to reduce extreme poverty and reduce the gap in per capita incomes between countries. Paul Ormerod has claimed that, in terms of differences in per capita income levels between countries, the world is now more equal than it was in 1950, and probably at around the same level that it was in 1850.

4.3.1 MEASURES OF DEVELOPMENT

What you need to know

Three dimensions of the Human Development Index (HDI) (education, health and living standards) and how they are measured and combined

Advantages and limitations of using the HDI to compare levels of development between countries and over time

Other indicators of development

What is development?

Development means many things to many people. It is fundamentally about people development over time. The **average income per head** in a high-income country is around $45,000, versus $800 in a low-income country

Nobel Economist Amartya Sen, writing in "Development as Freedom", sees development as concerned with improving the **freedoms** and **capabilities** of the disadvantaged, thereby enhancing the overall quality of life. Amartya Sen pursues the idea that human development provides an opportunity to people to free themselves from deep suffering caused by

- Early / premature mortality
- Persecution and intolerance
- Starvation / malnutrition
- Illiteracy

According to **Professor Ian Goldin** from Oxford University, development is about the ability to shape our own lives. It requires information, literacy, participation and capabilities.

Michael Todaro specified three objectives of development:

1. **Life sustaining goods and services:** to increase the availability and widen the distribution of basic life-sustaining goods such as food, shelter, health and protection services
2. **Higher incomes**: to raise standards of living, including, in addition to higher incomes, the provision of more jobs, better education, and greater attention to cultural and human values, all of which will serve not only to enhance material well-being but also to generate greater individual and national self-esteem
3. **Freedom to make economic and social choices:** to expand the range of economic and social choices available to individuals and nations by freeing them from servitude and dependence not only in relation to other people and nation-states but also to the forces of ignorance and human misery

Difference between growth and development
- **Economic growth**
    - A sustained rise in a country's productive capacity
    - An increase in real value of GDP / GNI per capita
    - Increases in the productivity of factors of production
- **Economic development**
    - Improvement in living standards
    - Progress in expanding economic freedoms
    - Sustained improvement in economic and social opportunities
    - Growth in personal and national capabilities

The Human Development Index (HDI)

The HDI focuses on longevity, basic education and income. It is a broad composite measure of improvements in people's lives – it is a weighted index. Each of the 3 measures is given a value between 0 and 1 (with 0 being very low development and 1 very high), and then an average is taken of the 3 composite indicators to give an overall measure of development. It can be expressed as a number between 0 and 100 (if the measure is multiplier by 100), or 0 and 1.

1. **Knowledge:** an educational component made up of two statistics – mean years of schooling (of those already in the workplace) and expected years of schooling (of those still in school)

2. **Long and healthy life:** a life expectancy component is calculated using a minimum value for life expectancy of 25 years and maximum value of 85 years
3. **A decent standard of living:** gross national income (GNI) per capita adjusted to purchasing power parity standard (PPP)
    - GNI (Gross National Income) is used because of the growing size of remittances across countries
    - Log of income is used in the HDI calculation because income is instrumental to human development, but higher incomes are assumed to have a declining extra contribution to human development

Countries with the lowest HDI values include Niger, South Sudan, Chad and Sierra Leone. Countries with the highest HDI values include Norway, Switzerland, Australia and Ireland.

Advantages and disadvantages of using the HDI

Disadvantages include:
- The standard HDI measure does not take into account **qualitative factors**, such as cultural identity and political freedoms (human security, gender opportunities and human rights)
- The GNI per capita figure – and consequently the HDI figure – takes no account of **income distribution**.
- If income is unevenly distributed, GNI per capita will be an inaccurate measure of people's **well-being**
- Purchasing power parity (PPP) values used to adjust GNI data change quickly and can be inaccurate
- Higher GNI may result in more spending on aspects that could reduce living standards e.g. polluting power stations rather than green energy production, or armaments

Advantages include:
- Relatively easy data to collect and compare
- As objective as possible – it could be difficult, for example, to come up with an accurate/reliable measure of more qualitative factors such as freedom of speech
- Measures such as longevity and education levels are indicative of other development factors
    - People tend to live longer if there is better access to doctors and healthcare, access to good sanitation and housing etc

Gender inequality and human development
- The Gender Inequality HDI rankings includes indicators that reflect the extent to which there are deep and persistent imbalances in economic, social and political freedoms for women and girls in developed and developing countries
- Rwanda has made significant progress in addressing gender inequalities – for example, in Rwanda, female lawmakers make up 61% of parliament, outperforming a world average of one woman in five

The difference between gender equality and gender equity
- **Gender equality** denotes women having the same opportunities in life as men, including the ability to participate in the public sphere.
- **Gender equity** denotes the equivalence in life outcomes for women and men, recognising their different needs and interests

Other indicators of development

There are many ways of measuring the extent, durability and progress of improvements in human economic development. Some of the key development metrics are summarised below:
- Changing structure of national output, trade and employment
- % of adult male and female labour in agriculture, % of arable land that is cultivated
- Access to clean water / improved sanitation facilities
- Energy consumption per capita / depth of hunger, incidence of malnutrition
- Fertility rates, natural rate of growth of population
- Prevalence of HIV, years of healthy life expectancy, child mortality
- Access to mobile cellular phone services, access to bank accounts, insurance
- Dependence of a country on foreign aid / levels of external debt
- High-technology exports (% of manufactured exports), patterns of exports
- Degree of primary export dependence
- Progress in achieving Sustainable Development Goals (SDGs)

Sustainable Development Goals (SDGs) from the United Nations
There are seventeen published sustainable development goals; intended to be achieved by 2030

Goal 1   End poverty in all its forms everywhere
Goal 2   End hunger, achieve food security and improved nutrition, promote sustainable agriculture
Goal 3   Ensure healthy lives and promote well-being for all at all ages
Goal 4   Ensure inclusive and equitable quality education and promote life-long learning opportunities for all
Goal 5   Achieve gender equality and empower all women and girls
Goal 6   Ensure availability and sustainable management of water and sanitation for all
Goal 7   Ensure access to affordable, reliable, sustainable, and modern energy for all
Goal 8   Promote sustained, inclusive and sustainable growth, full and productive employment and decent work for all
Goal 9   Build resilient infrastructure, promote inclusive and sustainable industrialisation and foster innovation
Goal 10 Reduce inequality within and among countries
Goal 11 Make cities and human settlements inclusive, safe, resilient and sustainable
Goal 12 Ensure sustainable consumption and production patterns
Goal 13 Take urgent action to combat climate change and its impacts
Goal 14 Conserve and sustainably use the oceans, seas and marine resources for sustainable development
Goal 15 Protect, restore and promote sustainable use of terrestrial ecosystems, sustainably manage forests, combat desertification, and halt and reverse land degradation and halt biodiversity loss and inclusive institutions at all levels
Goal 16 Promote peaceful and inclusive societies for sustainable development, provide access to justice for all
Goal 17 Strengthen the means of implementation and revitalise the global partnership for sustainable development

Exam Tip It is vital that you have good working knowledge of 2 or 3 developing economies from different parts of the world – keep your own notes and data.

4.3.2 FACTORS INFLUENCING GROWTH AND DEVELOPMENT

What you need to know

Impact of economic factors in different countries
- Primary product dependency and volatility of commodity prices
- Debt
- Savings gap: Harrod-Domar model
- Access to credit and banking infrastructure
- Foreign currency gap
- Education/skills
- Capital flight
- Absence of property rights
- Demographic factors
- Impact of non-economic factors in different countries

Exam Tip It is really important that you recognise that different countries have different reasons / explanations for their current level of development! Clearly, if there are different causes then countries will need a range of diverse policies to raise development.

Primary product dependency
Typically, countries at an earlier stage of development tend to export a narrower range of products. Many developing countries continue to have high dependence on extracting and exporting primary commodities. These economies are vulnerable to volatile global prices. There are significant risks from over-specialisation especially when the terms of trade from their main exports decline; as countries specialise more in primary commodities, it increases the supply of these commodities which, when coupled with relatively price inelastic demand for these goods, causes their price to fall quite significantly (and the revenue earned).

Resource-rich (factor input-driven) countries may suffer from the natural resource curse. High profits often fuel corruption, inequality and wasteful consumption as natural resources are depleted. High commodity prices can cause currency appreciation and may lead to the Dutch Disease / de-industrialisation. Often resource revenues are not used productively to diversify the economy and improve HDI outcomes through investment in education and health care. The end result is that many developing countries rich in natural resources often have slow rates of GDP growth and poor development scores.

The Prebisch-Singer Hypothesis

The Prebisch-Singer Hypothesis suggests that, over the long run, prices of primary goods such as coffee and cocoa decline in proportion to prices of manufactured goods such as cars and washing machines. The core idea behind the Prebisch-Singer hypothesis is as follows:

- There is likely to be a long-term decline in real commodity prices
- In part this is because the income elasticity of demand for commodities is lower than for manufactured goods
- This then worsens the terms of trade for primary exporters over time
- In this situation, countries might be better off focusing on import substitution policies which encourage rapid industrialisation and improved export diversification designed to make a country more resilient to price shocks

What is Dutch Disease?

Dutch Disease refers to the adverse impact of a sudden discovery of natural resources on the national economy via the **appreciation of the real exchange rate** and the decline in export competitiveness. If natural resources are found and extracted and if the world price of them is rising, then export revenues will increase and there will be increased investment into that sector. But the risk is that there is a corresponding loss of investment into other industries such as manufacturing businesses. And the surge in export incomes can cause an appreciation of the exchange rate which then makes other sectors trying to export less competitive in overseas markets. A worst-case scenario is when manufacturing industries in developing countries start to shrink well before it has reached middle-income status. This is known as premature de-industrialisation.

Strategies for reducing primary product dependency and price volatility

1. **Better government** – including more transparency and accountability to taxpayers so that it is clear how natural resource revenues are being spent
2. **Stabilisation fund / sovereign wealth fund** e.g. to fund human capital and infrastructure or to inject money into an economy when aggregate demand dips
3. **Higher taxes on natural resource profits** i.e. extracting resource rents and then reinvesting in the domestic economy to increase a country's supply-side capacity
4. **Buffer stock schemes** – these are designed in principle to reduce some of the effects of price volatility although most less developed countries have limited ability to influence the world prices of their key exports
5. **Diversification** including shifting resources into processing, light manufacturing and tourism – giving higher value added and making the economy less susceptible to external shocks

What is the savings gap?

- Savings are needed to help finance capital investment
- Many rich countries have excess savings, whereas in smaller low-income countries, extreme poverty make it almost impossible to generate sufficient savings to fund capital investment projects
- Furthermore, the financial / banking sector may be extremely underdeveloped in developing economies, and there may no guarantees provided by governments for depositors to get their money back in case of bank failure
- This increases reliance on foreign aid or borrowing from overseas (leading to higher external debt)
- This problem is known as the savings gap
- In sub Saharan Africa for example, savings rates of around 4.7% of GDP in 2023 compared to 27% on average for middle-income countries
- Low savings rates and poorly developed or malfunctioning financial markets then make it more expensive for developing country public and private sectors to get the funds needed for capital investment

Harrod Domar model of growth

The Harrod-Domar model stresses the importance of savings and investment. The rate of growth depends on:
- Level of national saving (S)
- The productivity of capital investment (capital-output ratio)

For example, if £100 worth of capital equipment produces each £10 of annual output, a capital-output ratio of 10 to 1 exists. When the quality of capital resources is high and when an economy can better apply capital inputs and appropriate technologies e.g. by using more advanced ideas, then the capital output ratio will improve.

The rate of growth of GDP = **savings ratio / capital output ratio.**

Role of higher savings

An increase in national savings leads to an increase in investment – which leads to a larger capital stock – which leads to an increase in real GNI – which leads to increased factor incomes – which in turn allows more households to save.

Importance of capital investment for developing countries

Investment is an important driver of growth for developing/emerging countries:
- Injection of demand for capital goods industries
- Creates positive multiplier effects
- Increased capital stock can increase rural productivity and therefore income per head and consumption in rural areas
- Investment in new machinery and factories supports economies of scale especially in new / infant industries
- It can help achieve export-led growth because of the increase in productive capacity

Foreign currency gaps

What is a foreign currency gap?

- Many developing countries face imbalance between inflows and outflows of currencies such as US $s and Euros.
- A foreign exchange gap happens when currency outflows exceed currency inflows. This can occur when:
    - A country is running a persistent current account deficit
    - There is an outflow of capital from investors in money and capital markets (this is known as capital flight)
    - There is a fall in the value of inflows of remittances from nationals living and working overseas

A key consequence of a foreign currency gap can be that a nation does not have enough foreign currency to pay for essential imports such as medicines, foodstuffs and critical raw materials and replacement component parts for machinery. In this way, a foreign currency shortage can severely hamper short run economic growth and also hurt development outcomes.

Options for developing countries wanting to attract external finance

Developing economies can draw on a range of external sources of finance, including **FDI, portfolio equity flows, long-term and short-term loans** (both private and public), **overseas aid**, and also **remittances** from migrants living and working overseas. Foreign direct investment remains the largest external source of finance for developing economies. It makes up nearly 40 percent of total incoming finance in developing economies as a group, but less than a quarter in the least developed nations, with a declining trend since 2012.

Capital flight

Capital flight is the uncertain and rapid movement of large sums of money out of a country. The UK Overseas Development Institute (ODI) defines capital flight as "the outflow of resident capital which is motivated by economic and political uncertainty." There could be several reasons linked to a lack of investor confidence:

1. Political turmoil / unrest / risk of civil conflict
2. Fears that a government plans to take assets under state control
3. Exchange rate uncertainty e.g. ahead of a possible devaluation
4. Fears over the stability of a country's financial system

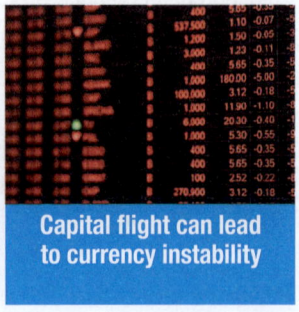

Foreign investors may take their money out of a country

Capital flight can lead to currency instability

Many billions of US$s each year are taken out of a country illegally especially in countries with persistently high levels of corruption. Capital flight can undermine the stability of the financial system and also lead to a weaker currency which in turn then increases the prices of essential imported goods such as components and food and it also makes it harder (more expensive) for a country to finance their external debts.

We tend to associate capital flight with countries where there are deep-rooted economic and political difficulties such as Russia, Pakistan, Nigeria and countries troubled by civil war. One policy to limit the amount of capital flight is for a government to introduce capital controls which control how much money people can take out of a country. However illegal capital outflows are much harder to stop.

Demographic factors

Demography is concerned with the **size** and **composition** of a population. Over time, demographic change can have a powerful impact on the growth and development prospects of advanced and emerging / developing countries alike.

During the past half century, the world has experienced an unprecedented increase in its population size. In 1960, roughly three billion people inhabited the planet; 50 years later, it was around seven billion – with almost one billion people added in the decade between 2000 and 2010. The World Bank projects that in the next 35 years, another 2.5 billion people will be added to the planet; over 90% of this increase in population size will be in developing countries.

Between 2018 and 2030, the **working age population** will grow by 552 million in low- and middle-income countries. In high income countries, the working-age population will decrease by 40 million people. The world population is projected to reach nearly 10 billion by 2050.

Life expectancy is rising - globally, life expectancy has risen by seven years. In some countries, that rise has been as much as 19 years, and since 1990, life expectancy has improved in 96% of countries. Back then, people born in 11 countries would not be expected to reach 50, yet this milestone was reached by every country in 2016.

Ageing populations and population decline

In a growing number of rich nations, **population growth is slowing down**, and, in some cases, there is negative natural population growth not offset by inward migration. In Japan for example, an **ageing population** combined with low female participation and low net inward migration is causing a contraction in the size of their active labour force. In countries such as Latvia and Bulgaria, the resident population is declining by more than 1 percent each year.

According to the OECD, "the ageing of the population in OECD countries, which is expected to continue in the next decades, may contribute to reduced innovation, reduced output growth and reduced real interest rates across OECD economies." Research published in 2017 suggested that an ageing population could lead to a slowdown in innovation. Societies may become considerably more risk-averse as their average age rises, which may have important consequences such as reducing investment in the stock market or the extent of self-employment.

The table below tracks a selection of high-income countries with a **high median age** and **high age-dependency ratio**.

		Population					Dependency ratio	
		Total		Average annual growth		Urban	Median age	(per 100 people ages 15–64)	
HDI rank	Country	(millions)		(%)		(%)	(years)	Young age (0–14)	Old age (65 and older)
		2024	2030	2005/2010	2015/2020	2024	2024	2024	2024
24	Japan	123.9	121.6	0.0	-0.2	92.0	49.5	21.0	48.0
30	Italy	58.9	58.1	0.3	-0.1	72.0	48.1	20.4	36.6
12	Finland	5.6	5.7	0.4	0.4	85.8	43.2	25.8	36.6
42	Portugal	10.6	9.9	0.2	-0.4	67.9	46.0	20.3	35.5
7	Germany	84.7	82.2	-0.2	0.2	77.8	46.7	21.7	33.7

The UK has an **ageing population**: there are around 12.8 million people of pensionable age today. Population projections predict that there will be 16.3 million people of pensionable age in the UK by 2041.

Possible microeconomic effects

1. Changing patterns of consumer demand in markets / affecting profits of businesses in particular sectors
2. Impact on government welfare spending and tax revenues e.g. health care for the elderly, treatment of chronic illness
3. Impact on housing market e.g. if people can live in their own homes for longer

Possible macroeconomic effects

1. Impact on the rate of growth of productivity and long-term GDP growth, for example, if there is an increase in the age-dependency ratio
2. Impact on business competitiveness if the median age continues to rise rapidly
3. Increased demand for state-funded health care including social care and a possible reduction in tax revenues if the active labour force contracts

Rapid population growth in developing countries

In many lower and middle-income countries, rising income per head can actually cause an increase in population growth. This is because higher incomes and consumption leads to improved access to health care and leads both to higher fertility and to lower infant and child mortality. Global population was around 3 billion in 1960. In 1987, it was over 5 billion. And as of 2024 there were about 7.95 billion people in the world.

Opportunities from rapid population growth

1. A young median age and fast natural population growth contributes to an expanding population of working age which can increase long-run aggregate supply (LRAS) causing an outward shift of the PPF.
2. Providing per capita incomes are rising, then population growth increases the size of domestic markets - encouraging economies of scale and increased capital investment spending by businesses.
3. More people in work leads to a widening of the tax base to help government finances.
4. Population growth and urbanisation tend to go together - population growth increases density and, alongside rural-urban migration, can lead to benefits from agglomeration economies. Urbanisation has been linked to stronger innovation and it also stimulates demand for new infrastructure which in turn creates jobs and creates positive multiplier effects.
5. The challenge of feeding a growing population can be a catalyst for research and development and innovation in farming designed to increase crop yields.

Risks and drawbacks from rapid population growth

1. A large number of young people entering the labour market creates challenges - not least in providing sufficient jobs in the formal economy to prevent a large increase in youth unemployment.
2. Fast-growing population holds back the annual growth of per capita incomes. Income is spread more thinly across large households which makes it harder to satisfy everyone's basic needs and wants and can lead to rising malnutrition.
3. Rapid population growth puts increasing pressure on the natural environment including demand for water and energy and can also threaten bio-diversity
4. High rates of rural-urban migration can lead to problems associated with urban density such as crime, the spread of disease and increased inequalities of income and wealth.

Brain drain effects

Some countries experience a **brain drain effect** which describes the movement of highly skilled or professional people from their own country to another country where they can earn more money. Brain drains can lead to **de-population.**

Consider the Baltic state of Latvia as an example; their population is forecast to contract by 200,000 people between 2017 and 2030, a fall of over 10%. Over the same period Ukraine may see a 3 million decline in their total population.

Disadvantages from a brain drain

1. Loss of human capital – this damages long-run supply-side potential and is a barrier to development
2. Loss of enterprising younger workers who might have started up businesses at home
3. Skills shortages affect HDI outcomes e.g. the emigration of skilled doctors, teachers and engineers
4. Risk of a fall in aggregate demand because of a smaller population
5. Depopulation make the country less attractive to inflows of foreign investment

Possible advantages from a brain drain
1. Remittances from emigrants flow back to increase a nation's gross national income (GNI)
2. People living overseas (the diaspora) may be able to help finance private sector capital projects in the future
3. Acquisition of human capital by working and studying in other countries e.g. learning languages, earning degrees – possibly leading to brain gains if they return to their country of origin
4. May help to offset the risks from rapid natural growth of population such as higher inflation and pressure on the built environment and natural resources

External debt

Many developing countries accumulate a growing amount of external debt. **External debt** is owed to external (overseas) creditors and examples of debt includes government bonds sold to foreign investors and private sector credit borrowed from foreign banks. The scale of external debt is usually measured as a % of a country's GNI.

External debt tends to rise when
1. A government is running a budget deficit and finances this by selling government bonds to overseas creditors
2. A country is running a sizeable current account deficit which is partly funded by borrowing from overseas institutions such as the IMF
3. Households and businesses borrow money in a foreign currency including mortgages and corporate bonds

Debt in itself is not necessarily a problem if the borrowing is being used to help fund capital investment projects which will ultimately increase a nation's productive potential and increase trend economic growth.

But there are risks with a developing country increasing the scale of external debt:
- Returns on investment might fall short of expectations especially if investment goes on projects not subject to a proper cost-benefit analysis
- If a country experiences a depreciation/devaluation of their exchange rate, the real value of the debt will increase making it harder to repay
- A recession can make it harder to meet the interest payments on debt since government tax revenues shrink
- If international investors become nervous about the ability of a government to repay external debt, then a country may suffer a credit-rating downgrade which will increase the interest rate needed to finance new loans

High levels of external debt combined with high interest rates lead to the problem of a country's interest payments being a high percentage of GNI and an even bigger percentage of their export earnings each year. This has led to pressure for debt relief policies involving some forms of **debt forgiveness** or **debt rescheduling** for the poorest countries.

Access to credit and banking

Improving access to basic financial services, such as a bank account, credit, and insurance, is a crucial step in improving people's lives. World Bank research finds that financial inclusion is on the rise globally, accelerated by mobile phones and the internet, but gains have been uneven across countries. Globally, 1.7 billion adults remain unbanked, yet two-thirds of them own a mobile phone that could help them access financial services. Half of all the adults in the world who lack bank accounts live in just seven countries.

The cost of finance and insurance in many of the least developed countries remains a structural problem: many people who have transaction accounts but whose incomes are low or irregular, rely on expensive solutions, such as payday lending, cheque-cashing services, or informal money-lenders to cover shortfalls in income.

Financial access connects people into the formal financial system, making day-to-day living easier and allowing them to build assets, mitigate shocks related to emergencies, illness, or injury, and make productive investments. It also makes it easier for a government to measure economic activity and collect in tax revenues needed to pay for public services.

Millions of the world's poorest people rely on informal loans often at high rates of interest. Millions find it tough to secure loans for businesses or to fund education and health care because they will have no collateral.

Infrastructure

Transport costs affect cost competitiveness

Unreliable and expensive power increases costs

Infrastructure consists of a spectrum of public, semi-public, and private goods. Public goods include access to safe drinking water and sanitation. Semi-public goods include networks providing electricity, roads, ports, and airports.

Infrastructure needs to be robust to cope with the effects of **rapid urbanisation** and **climate change**. According to the World Bank, over the next 35 years, urban populations are estimated to expand by an additional 2.5 billion people — this is almost double the population of China. For the first time in history, more people now live in cities than in rural areas. There is growing need for renewable energy infrastructure to build resilience to the effects of climate change.

How infrastructure gaps can limit economic growth and development

Infrastructure gaps:

- Increase supply costs for businesses – this causes higher prices – therefore hitting real incomes for consumers
- Reduces geographical mobility of labour causing higher structural unemployment (a labour market failure)
- Damages export competitiveness and limits intra-regional trade (trade within a cluster of countries)
- Can make a country less attractive to foreign direct investment (FDI) which might then slow economic growth
- Makes an economy vulnerable to climate change / natural disasters such as flooding and earthquakes
- Contributes to gender inequality
- Has a direct impact on basic human development e.g. having access to basic water and sanitation services

Education and skills – gaps in human capital

What is human capital?

Human capital is the **skill, knowledge, talent, experience and ability of workers**. Human capital can be increased through investment in education and training.

The quality of education differs strongly between and within different countries. Globally, more than 260 million children and youth are not in school and nearly 60 percent of primary school children in developing countries fail to achieve minimum proficiency in learning.

Poor human capital hits labour productivity and ability to harness/adapt to new technologies. Low productivity keeps wages down. Human capital deficiencies are closely linked to malnutrition. Better basic health care and nutrition helps to unlock improved human capital by avoiding brain impairment and the effects of stunted growth.

Absence of property rights

Why are property rights important for development?

1. Rights to own land and to establish businesses are seen as crucial for wealth creation e.g. private plots to farm
2. Protection of property rights is a major barrier to corruption
3. Property rights are important to tackle gender inequalities
4. Community ownership / management of natural resources can help overcome threats to eco-systems
5. Laws on patents are important to secure investment in research industries
6. Common rules encourage trade and investment between countries by reducing trade friction costs

Gender inequality as a barrier to growth and development

No society can achieve its potential without the full and equal participation of women and men. According to the UN Human Development Report: "All too often, women and girls are discriminated against in health, education, political representation, labour market, etc. with negative repercussions for development of their capabilities and their freedom of choice."

In 2024 the global labour force participation rate was just over 50 percent for women, but 80 percent for men.

- 62 million girls are not in school. Pregnancy and early marriage are key reasons for girls dropping out of school.
- Worldwide, over one hundred economies have laws that keep women out of certain jobs.
- Across the globe women occupy, on average, 27% of parliamentary seats in 2024, up from 12% in 1997.
- Gender inequality has cost the world an estimated $160 trillion, according to a new report.

There are huge differences in gender development outcomes when we contrast high development countries and the least developed nations. **Maternal mortality** is more than ten times higher; the **adolescent birth rate** is more than three times higher in LDCs and only a quarter of females in the least developed countries have at least **some secondary education** compared to nearly 90 per cent in countries ranked as reaching very high human development.

Non-economic factors that can affect development

Almost anything can affect development levels in an economy. Non-economic factors might include:
- Poor governance
- Degree of corruption
- Civil war and political unrest
- The geography of a country e.g. landlocked, mountainous etc

Corruption as a barrier to growth and development

Corruption is due to a **failure of governing institutions** which lack transparency about where tax revenues are coming from and how resources are spent. Corruption is defined broadly as the misuse of public power for private benefit. High levels of corruption damages long term growth and development in a number of ways:
- Deters foreign direct investment by increasing the cost of doing business
- Leads to allocative inefficiency i.e. diverting public resources for private gain, there are numerous extreme examples of extravagant wealth in economically less developed countries
- Government decisions are often unduly influenced by lobbying
- Contributes to income and wealth inequality and reduced progress in cutting the incidence of extreme poverty
- Causes a loss of trust i.e. a breakdown of social capital
- Leads to poorer development outcomes because governments are not collecting sufficient tax revenues

Exam Tip It is vital that you do not assume all governments in developing economies are corrupt. Mistakes or issues with public finances could stem from e.g. low levels of education, lack of funding for statistics collection and analysis, or lobbying from NGOs or TNCs.

Extension ideas: The economist Paul Collier has covered many of these factors in his book "The Bottom Billion". There is also some interesting coverage of these factors by Tim Marshall in his book Prisoners of Geography.

Example analysis and evaluation paragraphs: Examine the barriers that prevent economic development

Example KAA Point
The first barrier facing developing countries is **primary product dependency** - this is when the economy is dominated by primary sectors (typically **extraction of natural resources such as copper by the Democratic Republic of the Congo**). These are typically sectors where there is little opportunity for **value added** in processing and manufacturing. Technological advancement means that these industries are **capital intensive**, reducing the need for a large local workforce and limiting the need for investment in **human capital**. Workers in these industries often earn very low wages which limits progress in reducing **extreme poverty**.

Example Evaluation Point
However, the extent to which primary product dependency is harmful to development **depends on** the quality of governance and state capacity. For instance, states can act to diversify the economy using the windfall revenues and profits from primary products in the good years by investing in a **Sovereign Wealth Fund** (e.g. Norway) and a **Stabilisation Fund** set up by Ghana. Diversification also means that the workforce can work in industries with greater value added, such as the processing of oil, coffee and copper which will result in higher wages and per capita incomes and consumption which promotes development.

Example KAA Point
A second barrier to development is **capital flight**. This is when there is rapid, large-scale exit of financial capital due to a reduction in confidence. The exit of financial capital reduces the **supply of loanable funds** which then reduces access to credit for firms and governments. The resulting increased interest rates from the reduced supply of loans reduces borrowing by government and individuals. As a result, capital flight can lead to a fall in investment causing a contraction in AD, and thus an increase in demand deficient unemployment as GDP growth slows and firms are left with more spare capacity.

Example Evaluation Point
The extent to which capital flight poses a risk to development is dependent on how reliant countries are on liquid forms of capital inflows such as hot money/portfolio investment. This occurs when they are unable to attract FDI which is more stable and less susceptible to changes in investor sentiment. This is a problem that particularly affects lower-income countries. Additionally, developing nations without large foreign currency reserves will be especially affected from capital flight, as a central bank will be unable to defend the currency from depreciating.

4.3.3 STRATEGIES INFLUENCING GROWTH AND DEVELOPMENT

> **What you need to know**
>
> **Market-orientated strategies**
> - Trade liberalisation • Promotion of FDI • Removal of government subsidies • Floating exchange rate systems
> - Microfinance schemes • Privatisation
>
> **Interventionist strategies**
> - Development of human capital • Protectionism • Managed exchange rates • Infrastructure development
> - Promoting joint ventures with global companies • Buffer stock schemes
>
> **Other strategies**
> - Industrialisation: the Lewis model • Development of tourism • Fairtrade schemes • Overseas aid
> - Debt relief
>
> **Awareness of the role of international institutions and non-government organisations (NGOs)**
> - World Bank • International Monetary Fund (IMF) • NGO

Exam Tip This section on development policies mostly covers policies and ideas that you have already covered elsewhere in your A level course – but you must now apply what you already know to the context of developing economies!

Market-oriented strategies

Free-market approaches favour giving a larger role to **private sector enterprises** using **liberalisation of markets**, structural supply-side reforms to raise incentives for people and businesses with increased transparency for government also high on the policy agenda. Chile and Estonia are economies that have followed a free-market agenda for development.

Examples of market-led policies
- Fiscal discipline – emphasising greater control of government spending, budget deficits and national debt
- Reallocating state spending away from subsidies (e.g. minimum prices to farmers) towards health care, education and infrastructure
- Tax reforms – including widening the base of taxation and encouraging lower tax rates to raise enterprise and work incentives as a means of creating wealth
- Liberalising market interest rates i.e. letting financial markets allocate capital among competing uses
- Floating rather than fixed exchange rates – which implies an absence of central bank intervention
- Trade liberalisation via reductions in import tariffs and fewer forms of protectionism such as import quotas and other non-tariff barriers
- Privatisation i.e. moving state enterprises into the private sector

Trade liberalisation

Trade liberalisation involves a country lowering import tariffs and relaxing import quotas and other forms of protectionism. One of the aims of liberalisation is to make an economy **more open to trade and investment** so that it can then engage more directly in the regional and global economy. Supporters of free trade argue that developing countries can **specialise** in the goods and services in which they have a **comparative advantage**.

Consider the diagram below which shows the effects of removing an import tariff on vehicles.

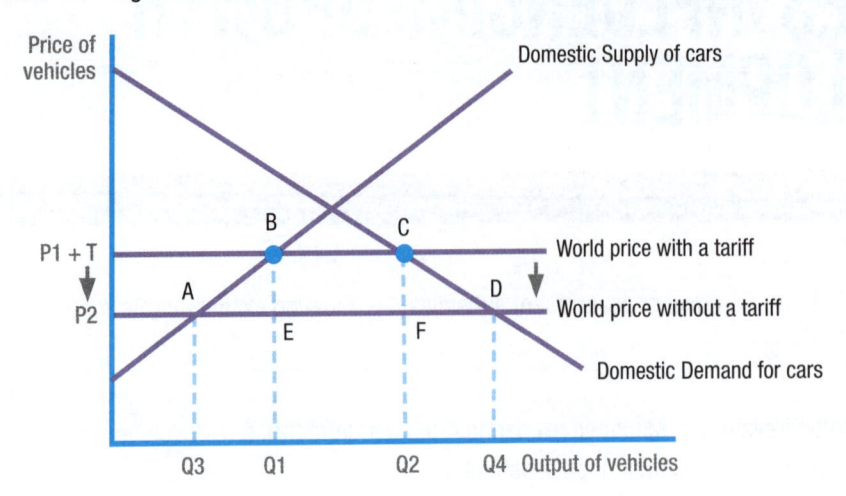

Trade liberalisation can have micro and macroeconomic effects:

Micro effects
- Lower prices for consumers / households which then increases their real incomes
- Increased competition – lower barriers to entry attracts new firms
- Improved efficiency – both allocative and productive
- Might affect the real wages of workers in affected industries

Macro effects
- Multiplier effects from higher export sales
- Lower inflation from cheaper imports – causing an outward shift of short run aggregate supply
- Risk of some structural unemployment / occupational immobility
- May lead initially to an increase in the size of a nation's trade deficit

Promotion of Foreign Direct Investment

Many countries rely on inflows of foreign direct investment (FDI) as a key source of aggregate demand and as a driver of real growth.

Exam Tip Make sure that you consider the possible effects of a rise in FDI on both **aggregate demand** and also **long run aggregate supply**.

Main gains from attracting inflows of FDI:
1. Improved infrastructure especially in power and transport sectors
2. Higher capital intensity / capital deepening i.e. more capital per worker which leads to higher productivity
3. Better training for local workers leading to improved human capital and less risk of structural unemployment
4. Investment grows a country's export capacity (e.g. via firms attracted into special economic zones)
5. Technology and know-how transfer, promoting diversification of the economy and reducing primary dependence
6. More competition in markets which then lowers prices for consumers and increases their real incomes
7. Creates new jobs leading to higher per capita incomes and increased household savings
8. FDI can promote a shift to higher productivity jobs and high value-added industries

Exam Tip The impact of foreign direct investment in a given country needs to be judged on a case-by-case basis.

What are the main risks from policies designed to attract investment into an emerging economy?
1. Multinationals wield power within host countries especially LEDCs and they can gain favourable laws and regulations
2. Foreign multinationals take advantage of weak laws on anti-competitive practices and environmental protection
3. Multinationals have been criticised for poor working conditions in foreign factories
4. Profits made in an LEDC are often repatriated to the host country
5. Imports of components/capital goods initially have a negative effect on a country's trade balance
6. Multinationals may only employ local labour in lower skilled jobs

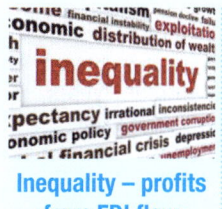

| Inequality – profits from FDI flow disproportionately to powerful elites | Many global corporations use tax avoidance techniques to increase their profits | Ethical standards from TNCs may be poor especially in mining, farming and textiles | Volatile / footloose FDI flows e.g. FDI is more volatile than remittance flows | Limited job creation effects / small spillover for local content suppliers | Monopsony power of TNCs who are able to negotiate highly favourable prices |

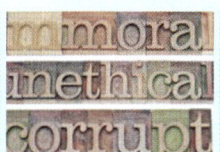

Policies designed to attract foreign direct investment

| Attractive rates of corporation tax | Soft loans and tax reliefs / subsidies | Trade and investment agreements e.g. TPP | Flexible labour force and skilled workers |
| Creation of Special Economic Zones | High quality critical infrastructure | Open capital markets for remitted profits | Attraction of relatively low unit labour costs |

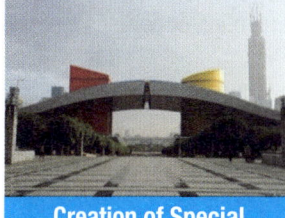

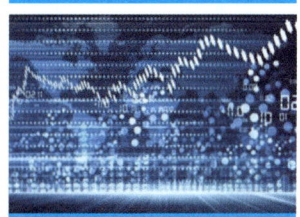

Removal of government subsidies

In many developing countries, a sizeable number of producers especially in farming and energy receive subsidies or some other form of government financial support such as a guaranteed minimum price. Economists who support intervention to promote development argue that subsidies can play an important role in improving (for example) farm incomes which then leads to higher capital investment and supports innovation and improved productivity in the long run. Subsidies are also a way of encouraging increased production to help overcome the challenges of malnutrition among the poor and they help to generate surpluses for export.

However, free-market critics of government subsidies argue that:
1. Subsidies distort the working of the price mechanism.
2. Subsidies can stifle innovation because producers are less reliant on innovation as a way of making more profit.
3. Producers / growers can become "subsidy-dependent" in the long run and there is also the risk of corruption syphoning off financial support to those who don't need it.
4. From an environmental point of view, subsidies can lower the incentive for producers to improve efficiency, instead they are rewarded by increasing the intensification of farming which can lead to deforestation, a loss of bio-diversity and increased water scarcity. Farmers may overuse fertilisers or pesticides, which can then result in soil degradation which reduces the maximum sustainable yield in the long run.

Free-market economists make the case for lowering / eliminating subsidies paid to consumers. For example, many developing countries continue to use food-price subsidies or controls in a bid to improve nutrition. Whether this works or not is open to question as households might substitute some of their budget towards foods with less nutritional content because a subsidy effectively increases their real incomes.

Energy subsidies are widely adopted in developing countries - the IMF recently estimated that the value of energy subsidies to consumers amounted to nearly 3% of global GDP. Economists concerned about environmental threats from climate change would make the case for getting rid of these subsidies so that the price of energy accurately reflects the externalities involved.

There is also a case for cutting subsidies because of the high opportunity cost - perhaps government spending on subsidies might be better allocated to education, health services and public infrastructure?

Floating exchange rate systems

The choice of exchange rate system is an important part of macroeconomic policy for developing countries. Over many years, there has been a gradual shift among developing/emerging countries away from fixed (pegged) currency regimes towards managed floating or free-floating systems. Managed floating remains the most common.

Some of the arguments for choosing a floating exchange rate are summarised below:

1. A floating exchange rate can be helpful for countries exposed to external economic shocks. For example, Poland operates with a floating currency (the Zloty) inside the EU Single Market. When the global financial crisis erupted in 2007-08 and the wider European economy went into recession, the Polish zloty depreciated heavily against the Euro and the US dollar. This helped the Polish economy stabilise since their exports were now more competitive. In contrast, Greece was locked into the single currency and could not rely on a depreciation to restore some lost competitiveness

2. Floating exchange rates mean that a country's central bank does not have to intervene to change the currency's price. This means that they do not have to maintain large reserves of gold and other foreign currencies.

3. Many developing countries have become more open to trade in goods and services and inflows and outflows of investment. Maintaining a floating exchange rate implies that capital controls will not be used to limit the inflow and outflow of currency and this in turn may make a country more attractive to foreign investment

4. Floating currencies are not necessarily volatile ones and allowing market forces to determine the price means that a government/central bank is not using up foreign currency reserves to defend a fixed exchange rate that the market has decided is not sustainable

Revision Tip For the downsides of floating exchange rates and the case for managed intervention or perhaps a pegged currency system, go back to the section on exchange rate systems.

Evaluation
- A floating currency might be more appropriate for a country with a low trade to GDP ratio since exchange rate fluctuations would have less of an impact on the trade balance and the inflation rate.
- We have to consider whether a country has the size and reserves to be able to control their own currency. Many smaller EU nations including the island countries of Cyprus and Malta have chosen to join the single European Currency.
- An economy with one dominant trade partner might decide that the advantages of a pegged currency outweigh come of the possible gains from currency flexibility

Microfinance schemes

The world's poor are exposed to irregular income flows, and their needs are irregular too – ranging from unforeseen medical bills to having to pay more when food prices rise unexpectedly. Microfinance refers to a large number of different financial products, including but not exclusive to

1. **Micro-credit** - the provision of small-scale loans to the poor for example by credit unions
2. **Micro-savings** – for example, voluntary local savings clubs provided by charities
3. **Micro-insurance** - especially for people and businesses not traditionally served by commercial insurance businesses - a safety net to prevent people from falling back into extreme poverty
4. **Remittance management** – managing remittance payments sent from one country to another including for example transfer payments made through mobile phone solutions

The concept of microcredit was first introduced in Bangladesh by **Muhammad Yunus** who started the Grameen Bank more than 30 years ago with the aim of reducing poverty by providing small loans to the country's rural poor.

A key feature of micro-finance has been the targeting of women on the grounds that compared to men, they perform better as clients of micro finance institutions and that their participation has more desirable long-term development outcomes. The **Grameen Bank** approach initially focused on small groups 'lending circles' of largely female entrepreneurs from the poorest level in the society. This became the widely accepted view of what micro finance is. In reality there are thousands of commercial microfinance institutions (MFIs) including some large international operators.

Benefits of micro-credit
- Helps overcome the savings gap which limits entrepreneurship
- Encourages entrepreneurship especially social enterprises
- Targeted at women entrepreneurs
- High rates of repayment because the system is built on social capital / trust

Disadvantages of micro-credit
- High interest rates
- Low success rate for new small businesses
- Alleged forcible collection of debt in many villages – hard to monitor
- Perhaps relatively ineffective compared to the impact of migrant remittances and foreign direct investment

Privatisation

Privatisation is the transfer of a business, industry or service from **public to private ownership**.

Benefits of privatisation
1. Private companies have a profit incentive to cut costs and be more productively efficient and raise efficiency.
2. Government gains revenue from the sale of assets and no longer has to support a potentially loss-making industry.
3. If a state monopoly is replaced by a number of firms this extra contestability in an industry will lead to lower prices which helps to increase the real incomes of poorer households.
4. The competitiveness of the macro economy may also improve especially if privatisation leads to increased investment and benefits from economies of scale. Improved competitiveness will drive higher exports and long run GDP growth.

Drawbacks / disadvantages from privatisation
1. Social objectives are given less importance because privately-owned firms are driven by the profit motive.
2. Some activities are best run by the state operating in the public interest because they are strategic parts of the economy e.g. water supply, steel and railways and have the characteristics of a natural monopoly.
3. Government loses out on dividends from any future profits.
4. Public sector assets are often sold cheaply, and the privatisation process may suffer from corruption.
5. Privatisation leads to job losses as firms increase their efficiency – this increases the risk of poverty for those affected.
6. Unless privatised corporations are regulated effectively, there is a risk of creating private monopolies who use their market power to increase prices and profits which can have a regressive effect on the distribution of income.

Interventionist Strategies

Interventionist policies involve many different types of government intervention in markets designed to correct for multiple market failures, influence patterns of trade and investment and address some of the root causes of extreme poverty and inequality. Supporters of interventionist strategies believe in the concept of a developmental state where the government can be an active and positive force in driving sustainable and inclusive growth and development.

Some of the key possible roles for the state (government) are summarised below:
- Basic (universal) income and health care
- Accessible and affordable education of good quality
- Infrastructure especially in telecommunications, health and transport
- Core public goods that the free-market under-provides
- Institutions of governance (including judiciary)
- Public-private partnerships in supporting urbanisation
- Smarter regulation e.g. building codes, regulation of monopoly power
- Welfare provision to provide a basic social safety net and also encourage saving
- Progressive taxation and state spending to reduce inequality of income and wealth

Development of human capital

The World Bank defines human capital as "the knowledge, skills, and health that people accumulate over their lives, enabling them to realise their potential as productive members of society." Human capital is regarded as complementary to investment in physical capital such as new buildings, plant and equipment and the latest technology.

Differences in productivity and per capita incomes are strongly linked to variations in the quality and quantity of human capital available in a country. Research has found that between 10 and 30 percent of per capita GDP differences is attributable to cross-country differences in human capital.

According to the World Bank, in poorer countries, almost a quarter of children under five are malnourished, and 60 percent of primary school students fail to achieve even a rudimentary education. Worldwide, more than 260 million children and youth are not in school.

Interventions to improve human capital might include

1. Strategies to improve nutrition and reduce the extent of stunted growth among young people. An example is the use of conditional cash transfers: Shombhob, a conditional cash transfer piloted in Bangladesh, has been found to reduce wasting among children aged 10-22 months and improve mothers' knowledge about the benefits of breastfeeding.
2. Other health interventions can also increase school attendance - a famous study in Kenya by economist Esther Duflo found that deworming in childhood reduced school absences while raising wages in adulthood by as much as 20 percent. A project in Nepal to improve basic sanitation led to a measured decline in anaemia among the young.
3. Increased investment in primary and secondary schooling - including policies to improve the quality of teaching and access to online education.
4. Incentives to attract an inflow of skilled migrant workers and curb 'brain drains' of highly qualified people - there are more Sudanese doctors working in London than Sudanese doctors working in Sudan.
5. Investment in training to re-skill people at risk of unemployment from the fast-changing pattern of employment including robotics, automation and artificial intelligence.
6. Cash transfer interventions can increase demand for education especially among the poorest families who must make hugely difficult decisions about how to spend a meagre budget.

Building human capital may also require behavioural interventions to address social and cultural norms that often prevent young people from starting or completing different grades of education.

> **Revision Tip** It is important to realise that interventions to build human capital can take several years to have a significant impact on productivity, competitiveness, economic growth and poverty reduction. The impact of each intervention needs to be subjected to a rigorous cost-benefit analysis. Interventions in one country are not necessarily as effective in another as all developing countries are different.
>
> Interventions are often hampered by inefficient bureaucracy which can lead to government failure.

Protectionism

A reality of the global trading system is that average import tariffs are higher when imposed by developing countries than those implemented by advanced, high-income nations. To what extent are protectionist policies such as tariffs, quotas, domestic subsidies and other trade barriers effective in supporting growth and development for lower and middle-income countries?

Main arguments/justifications for protectionism

1. Import substitution - trade barriers can be designed to protect fledgling domestic industries that have not yet achieved sufficient economies of scale to become cost and price competitive in international markets. The infant industry argument is often used as justification for tariffs that increase the prices of substitute products in strategically important industries.
2. Need to raise tax revenues - import duty revenues can be a useful source of tax revenues for developing countries especially when per capita incomes and formal employment is low which then limits the tax take from the domestic economy.
3. Tariffs can be justified as a response to alleged dumping of products into a country i.e. selling at a price below cost. Dumping can have a serious impact on the profits, investment and employment in those industries affected.
4. Tariffs might also be a retaliatory response to allegations that a country has used a competitive devaluation of their currency to make their exports more price competitive.

However, there are also risks for developing countries if they maintain high tariffs on imported goods and services:

1. Tariffs may protect jobs in some industries e.g. car making but have damaging effects elsewhere because they increase the prices of key imported raw materials, components and capital technologies.
2. Revenues raised by tariffs might only be a small percentage of total government revenue and lost jobs in other sectors will diminish the net effect on these revenues.
3. There is always the risk of retaliatory action by other countries - a good recent example was the tit-for-tat trade war between the United States and China.
4. Protectionist tariffs risk causing a loss of competition for domestic firms which eventually leads to lower productivity, less innovation and weaker competitiveness.
5. Tariffs increase prices for consumers leading to higher inflation, reduced real incomes and an increased risk of poverty for poorer households.
6. Protectionist subsidies for domestic firms can cost a government a lot of money leading to an increased budget deficit and rising national debt.

Managed exchange rates

A managed-floating currency when the central bank may choose to intervene in the foreign exchange markets to affect the value of a currency to meet specific macroeconomic objectives. For example, the central bank might attempt to bring about a depreciation to:

- Improve the balance of trade in goods and services / improve the current account position
- Reduce the risk of a deflationary recession - a lower currency increases export demand and increases the domestic price level by making imports more expensive
- Rebalance the economy away from domestic consumption towards exports and investment
- Sell foreign currencies to overseas investors as a way of reducing the size of government debt

Or to bring about an appreciation of the currency
- To curb demand-pull inflationary pressures
- To reduce the prices of imported capital and technology

Overall, one key aim of managed floating currencies is to **reduce the volatility of exchange rates**. This is because big fluctuations in the external value of a currency can increase investor risk and perhaps damage business confidence. If the risk for example of overseas investors buying a government's bonds rises, then they may demand a higher interest rate (or yield) on those bonds as compensation.

Managed floating exchange rates might also be used as a tool for a government to restore or improve the price competitiveness of exporters in global markets or perhaps respond to an external economic shock

Latest IMF classification of countries using a managed floating system:
Albania, Argentina, Armenia, Brazil, Colombia, Georgia, Ghana, Guatemala, Hungary, Iceland, India, Indonesia, Israel, Kazakhstan, Korea, Moldova, New Zealand, Paraguay, Peru, Philippines, Romania, South Africa, Thailand, Turkey, Uganda, Ukraine, Uruguay

IMF classification of countries using a free-floating currency:
Australia, Canada, Chile, Japan, Mexico, Norway, Poland, Russia, Sweden, United Kingdom, United States, European Union (Euro)

Exam Tip To manage a floating currency, the central bank needs to have sufficient **reserves of foreign currency** available should it need to intervene. There are also risks involved in changing domestic interest rates to have an impact in currency markets. For example, higher interest rates designed to attract hot money inflows and cause a currency appreciation might also have the effect of reducing consumer demand and cutting planned business investment. Remember to bring together a range of economic ideas and concepts when considering the impact of development policies!

Infrastructure development

Closing the infrastructure gap is now crucial in nearly all countries but especially emerging countries who want to make progress towards meeting the UN's Sustainable Development Goals (SDGs), bring down extreme poverty, improve their export capacity and address numerous environmental challenges. Infrastructure is critical for economic and social development the world over. Consider for example two specific sustainable development goals:

- SDG 6: "Ensure availability and sustainable management of water and sanitation for all"
- SDG 7.1: "Ensure access to affordable, reliable, sustainable and modern energy for all"

We can see below how much needs to be done in many developing countries, many of them in sub Saharan Africa and East Asia.

Proportion of population with access to a piped on-premises water supply and improved sanitation, 2021

Democratic Republic of Congo 40%

Ethiopia 39%

Rwanda 46%

Source: World Bank

Proportion of population with electricity access, 2021

Democratic Republic of Congo 19.1%

Ethiopia 51.1%

Rwanda 46.6%

Source: World Bank

For many countries there is insufficient investment in infrastructure. In part this is because of the enormous up-front financial commitment and the many years before the full benefits of new projects show fruit. The savings gap in many lower and middle-income nations makes financing big capital projects problematic and full of risk and the result can be a lack of investment which ultimately hampers growth and affects people's everyday lives. Attracting foreign direct investment to help fund and build infrastructure has become a common feature for many developing countries. The Chinese One Belt One Road initiative is an example of a hugely ambitious project stretching across many countries that could have a transforming impact but there are risks involved in relying too heavily on overseas capital.

Joint ventures with global companies

A joint venture (JV) is a separate business entity created by two or more parties, involving shared ownership, returns and risks. Joint ventures provide an opportunity for developing countries to acquire specific expertise in industries that they are hoping will be a new source of comparative advantage in the years ahead. For global companies, a joint venture can be a quicker way of securing access to new markets that were previously closed or subject to some form of protectionist policy.

Examples of recent joint ventures

- In 2022, India's Tata motors entered into a joint venture with France's Peugeot to manufacture cars in India
- In 2023, US pharma company Pfizer and Indian pharma company Dr Reddy's formed a joint venture to develop and sell new medicines in India

Buffer Stock Schemes

One way to smooth out fluctuations in prices is to operate price support schemes e.g. through the use of buffer stocks. Buffer stock schemes seek to stabilise the market price of agricultural products by:

- Buying up supplies when harvests are plentiful
- Selling stocks onto the market when supplies are low

In theory, buffer stock schemes will be profit making, since they buy up stocks of the product when the price is low and sell them onto the market when the price is high. However, they do not work well in practice, many buffer stock schemes have collapsed, and they can only work effectively for storable commodities.

> **Revision Tip** Buffer stock schemes provide an ideal opportunity for you to use the supply & demand analysis covered in Theme 1 microeconomics. Make sure that you thoroughly revise your notes on demand / supply and associated elasticities!

Buffer stock basic analysis:

The upper target price is designed to protect consumers from very high prices. The lower target price is designed to support farmers/growers when the market price is heading lower.

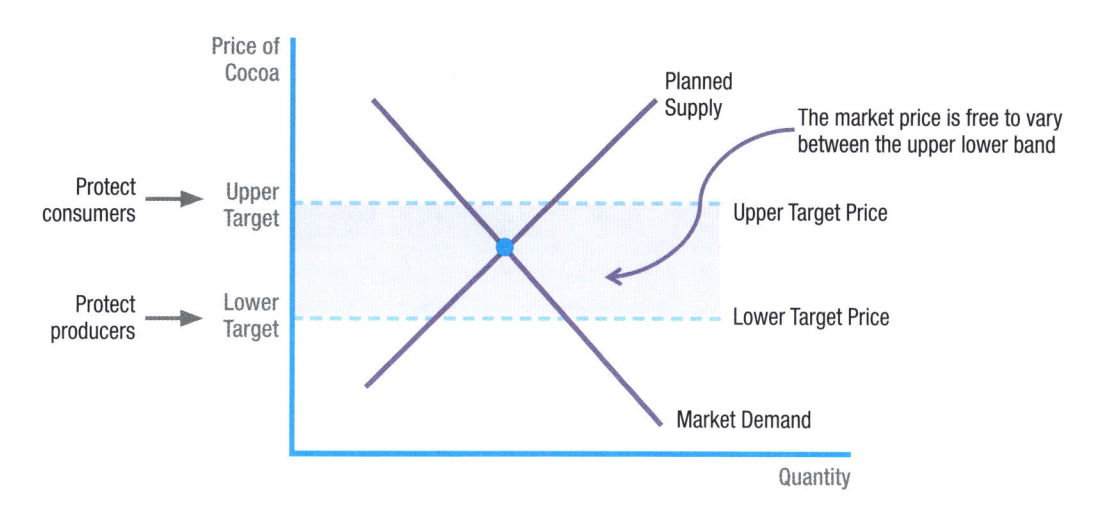

In the diagram to the right, actual supply (S1) is greater than planned supply leading to a surplus. If there is a run of good harvests, then stockpiles can build to high levels. Intervention purchases helps to drive the market price higher again.

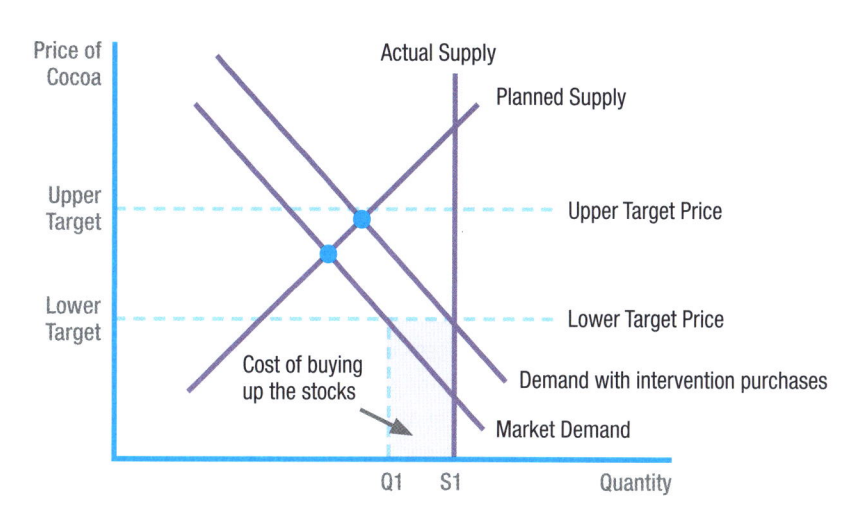

Arguments for and against a buffer stock scheme

The success of a buffer stock scheme ultimately depends on the ability of those managing a scheme to correctly estimate the average price of the product over a period of time.

Arguments for a buffer stock scheme
1. Lower risk of extreme food poverty for poorest consumers
2. More stable incomes and profits for farmers
3. Helps macroeconomic stability / investment
4. Buffer stock ought to be self-financing

Arguments against a buffer stock scheme
1. Buffer stock may not be large enough to change the market price
2. Setting a high price for farmers often causes rising surpluses i.e. a misallocation of resources
3. High costs of storage and falling quality of product (which might then have to be sold at discounted prices)
4. Many buffer stock schemes fail because of poor administration/corruption

Primary product dependence - alternatives to buffer stock schemes
- Strong evaluation involves considering alternative policies to stabilise prices and incomes for farmers
- In the long term, investment in capital goods such as irrigation and wider access to affordable insurance can be powerful
- So too are policies to reduce dependency on any one particular crop (see top of next page)

| Mobile technology to help farmers |  Encourage processing / branding by farmers |  Improved basic storage facilities + irrigation |  Micro insurance policies for poorer farmers |

Other strategies

Lewis model of industrialisation

Arthur Lewis put forward a development model of a **dual economy,** consisting of rural agricultural and urban manufacturing sectors. Initially, the majority of labour is employed upon the land, which is a fixed resource. Labour is a variable resource and, as more labour is put to work on the land, diminishing marginal returns eventually set in: there may be insufficient tasks for the marginal worker to undertake, resulting in reduced marginal product (output produced by an additional worker) and **underemployment.**

Urban workers, engaged in manufacturing, tend to produce a higher value of output than their agricultural counterparts. The resultant higher urban wages (Lewis stated that a 30% premium was required) might therefore tempt surplus agricultural workers to migrate to cities and engage in manufacturing activity. High urban profits would encourage firms to expand and hence result in further rural-urban migration. The Lewis model is a model of structural change since it outlines the development from a traditional economy to an industrialised one.

Countries such as Bangladesh, Malaysia and Vietnam have developed light manufacturing – by building textiles and garment industries – to add momentum to the process of industrialisation but much of sub Saharan Africa lags the rest of the world in terms of the contribution that manufacturing makes to national GDP. On average, across the continent, manufacturing only represents about 10 percent of total GDP in Africa, lagging behind other developing regions. Africa's share of world manufacturing exports is less than 1%. Ethiopia, Rwanda and Tanzania are three countries that have made sizeable progress in establishing scaled manufacturing sectors with growing export capacity whereas Nigeria and South Africa have seen declining growth in their industrial economy.

Is rapid industrialisation always the right approach for sustaining growth and development?

1. Whilst much manufacturing remains labour-intensive, the rapid adoption of robots and other automated processes can limit the scale of new job opportunities for people moving to urban areas where industries are concentrated
2. Successful manufacturing strategies often have close links back to farming and extractive sectors e.g. developing processing capabilities for farmers who grow fruit. Kenya has established a cut-flower processing industry that employs over 200,000 people and contributes more than $1 billion worth of exports each year
3. Light manufacturing does not always add a great deal of value added to production especially low-level assembly tasks. Countries might do better in the long run if they also invest in building human capital in industries such as research, engineering and design.
4. There are drawbacks from rapid urbanisation especially if a country does not have the infrastructure to cope with high rates of rural-urban migration.

Development of tourism

Travel and tourism generates over 9 percent of global gross domestic product and nearly 300 million jobs globally. There is a fierce debate about the long-term consequences of tourism - what role can tourism play in growth and development? Can travel to less developed countries do more harm than good?

Countries with highest % of GDP linked to tourism

Share of total GDP

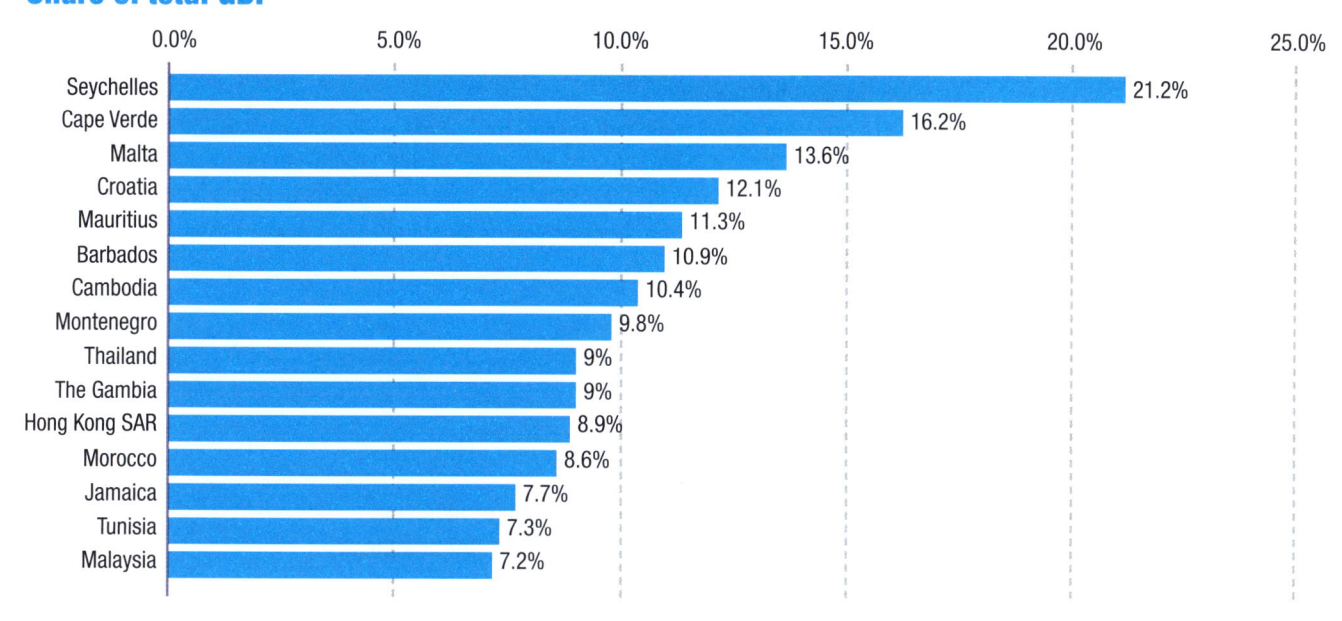

Country	%
Seychelles	21.2%
Cape Verde	16.2%
Malta	13.6%
Croatia	12.1%
Mauritius	11.3%
Barbados	10.9%
Cambodia	10.4%
Montenegro	9.8%
Thailand	9%
The Gambia	9%
Hong Kong SAR	8.9%
Morocco	8.6%
Jamaica	7.7%
Tunisia	7.3%
Malaysia	7.2%

Benefits of tourism for growth and development
1. Employment creation, tourism is a labour intensive industry.
2. Employs a significantly higher % of women helping to increase female labour market participation
3. Export earnings - tourism is a service industry – it helps to generate foreign exchange
4. An important source of diversification for many smaller countries – reducing primary dependency
5. Raises aggregate demand – possibly creating local and regional income-multiplier effects
6. Accelerator effects from investment in tourism infrastructure and services such as airlines and telecoms

Critical evaluation of expanding tourism
1. Exploitation of local labour by overseas TNCs, (e.g. consider the rapid growth of the sex industry in many countries)
2. Many workers in tourism are migrants suffering from poor employment conditions such as low wages/long hours
3. Outflow of profits from foreign-owned tourist resorts, many resorts have few locally-owned hotels
4. All-inclusive deals tend to ignore the local economy (see recent protests in the Canary islands)
5. Negative externalities from construction projects such as congestion, waste, pressure on the natural environment.
6. Rising property prices makes housing less affordable for local people
7. Deepening pressures on local cultures from westernisation, the doubtful benefits of slum-tourism and concerns with security and health
8. Tourism can be a highly cyclical industry vulnerable to global economic and political shocks

Tourism is becoming more significant for many of the world's least developed countries.

Fairtrade schemes

One of the driving forces behind the founders of Fairtrade was a desire to correct for multiple market failures in industries for many primary sector commodities. These failures included the effects of monopsony power among transnational food processors and food manufacturers which often led to farmers in some of the world's poorest countries receiving an inequitably low and unsustainable price for their products. A grower will be able to receive a Fairtrade licence if it can improve working conditions, better pay and guarantees of environmental sustainability

The key aims of Fairtrade are to:
- Guarantee a higher / premium price to certified producers
- Achieve greater price stability for growers
- Improve production standards

The Fairtrade movement has critics

1. Impact on non-participating farmers: some claim that by encouraging consumers to buy their products from Fairtrade sources, this cuts demand for farmers in poorer nations not covered by the Fairtrade label thereby worsening the risk of extreme poverty.
2. Who captures the gains from Fairtrade coffee? There is some evidence that a large part of the premium price goes to processors and distributors rather than the farmers themselves.
3. Others argue that the fundamental causes of poverty are not really addressed by Fairtrade. Greater investment needs to be made in raising farm productivity, reducing vulnerability to climate change, and reaching multi-lateral trade agreements between countries to reduce import tariffs and improve access for poor countries into the markets of rich advanced nations.
4. Other investment might be better targeted at encouraging farmers to establish producer co-operatives of their own and create their own branded products selling direct to consumers.

Overseas aid

Types of Overseas Development Assistance (Aid)

1. Bilateral aid: from one country to another
2. Multilateral aid: channelled through international bodies such as the United Nations
3. Project aid: direct financing of projects for a donor country
4. Technical assistance: funding of expertise of various types including engineering / medicine
5. Humanitarian aid: emergency disaster relief, food aid, refugee relief and disaster preparedness
6. Soft loans: a loan made to a country on a concessionary basis that offers a lower rate of interest
7. Tied aid: projects tied to suppliers in the donor country
8. Debt relief: cancellation, rescheduling, refinancing of a country's external debts

Exam Tip You should ensure that when discussing /evaluating aid that you consider the different types of aid i.e. not all aid is the same! By considering different types of aid, you can compare and contrast their effectiveness, thus gaining valuable evaluation marks.

Benefits of overseas aid

1. Helps to overcome the savings gap and aid can help stabilise post-conflict environments and disaster recovery.
2. Project aid can fast-forward investment in critical infrastructure – eventually leading to higher productivity.
3. Long-term aid for health and education projects – this builds human capital and stronger social institutions.
4. Targeted aid might add around 0.5% to the annual growth rate of the poorest countries - this benefits donor countries too as trade grows.

Risks / drawbacks from high levels of overseas aid

1. Poor governance - aid might leave the recipient country. It can finance corruption by ruling political elites.
2. Lack of transparency – hundreds of $m is spent on aid consultants and developed country non-governmental organisations.
3. Dependency culture – one aid paradox is that aid tends to be most effective where it is needed least – it may harm an entrepreneurial culture.
4. Aid may lead to a distortion of market forces and a loss of economic efficiency and might cause higher inflation.

The effectiveness of overseas aid needs to be monitored carefully so that each $ of aid is properly targeted to have a favourable effect. Aid may work more when targeted at low income countries and perhaps when it is made partially conditional on a government implementing some economic reforms. Aid does save lives – there is a measurable impact for example of aid projects designed to reduce mortality from HIV & Aids.

Debt relief

External debt is owed to external (overseas) creditors. Examples include government bonds sold to foreign investors and private sector credit from foreign banks. The scale of external debt is usually measured as a % of a country's GNI.

External debt can be a severe constraint on growth and development – often, the interest on existing debt takes up a large percentage of a nation's export revenues or annual tax revenues. These debt repayments have an opportunity cost; they might be better used in supporting development policies.

What is debt relief?

- Debt relief involves the cancellation, rescheduling, or refinancing of a nation's external debts.

- Many of the world's poorest countries have high levels of external debt owed to other governments, institutions such as the IMF and foreign companies, banks and individuals.
- The Heavily Indebted Poor Countries Initiative (HIPCI) is an initiative to provide debt relief to heavily indebted low-income countries.
- Debt relief agreements are often conditional on the host country introducing structural economic reforms.

The case for offering debt relief

1. High debt and the interest payments on debt can further impoverish the most vulnerable people in poor countries – debt relief is an appropriate form of aid for countries who lack access to global capital markets.
2. Poor countries highly dependent on exports of primary commodities are exposed to global economic shocks which can damage their export revenues and take them further into external debt. There is a moral argument for helping.
3. Debt relief can be made partially conditional on governments introducing economic and social reforms.

Arguments against extensive debt relief

1. Moral hazard argument – governments will spend and borrow more – perhaps recklessly – if they know/expect that some of their debts will be written off in the future – this increases the risk of government failure.
2. If governments ran better macroeconomic policies e.g. to control inflation and state borrowing, then the interest rates charged on new loans would fall making the repayment of debt less costly.

The World Bank

The World Bank comprises two institutions managed by member countries: the International Bank for Reconstruction and Development (IBRD) and the International Development Association (IDA). The IBRD aims to reduce poverty in middle-income and credit-worthy poorer countries. The IDA focuses exclusively on the world's poorest countries.

The World Bank

- Provides grants and low interest loans
- Offers policy advice and technical assistance to developing countries
- Co-ordinates projects with governments

Critics of the World Bank argue that the institution is risk averse, hugely over-staffed and overly sensitive to criticisms of their flagship projects and with multi-million-dollar expense accounts in stark contrast to their original mission.

International Monetary Fund (IMF)

The International Monetary Fund (IMF) has played a prominent role in world financial affairs in the post-Second World War period. In the 1950s and 1960s, its main purpose was to support the system of fixed exchange rates. Since then its activities have evolved to embrace developing economies and both banking and sovereign debt crises.

The International Monetary Fund (IMF)

- IMF was founded at the Bretton Woods conference in 1944
- The IMF works to foster global monetary cooperation, secure financial stability, facilitate global trade, promote high employment and sustainable economic growth, and reduce poverty around the world
- The IMF provides financing to its members when they are suffering economic difficulties
- Financial assistance can come in the form of conditional loans or training
- Emerging market countries argue that the IMF requires reform given the changing balance of power in the world economy

Key roles for the IMF

1. Promote international monetary co-operation
2. Facilitate the expansion of international trade
3. Provide exchange stability
4. Make resources available to members experiencing balance of payments difficulties

NGOs

An NGO is any not-for-profit voluntary group – it can operate on a local, regional, or international scale. NGOs often operate on a small scale in developing countries. They frequently work in the areas of environmental improvement, community development, and human rights – there have been notable interventions from NGOs in the removal of landmines in previously war-torn countries (e.g. Cambodia), gender equality and women's rights, and raising awareness of 'blood diamonds'. Choose two or three NGOs that operate in countries / areas that you might be interested in, and investigate their work!

4.4.1 ROLE OF FINANCIAL MARKETS

What you need to know

To facilitate saving
To lend to businesses and individuals
To facilitate the exchange of goods and services
To provide forward markets in currencies and commodities
To provide a market for equities

Money, capital and foreign exchange markets

For the purposes of your Edexcel A-level, you do not need to know about the money markets and capital markets in any detail (although you do need to understand foreign exchange markets!), and you are unlikely to see questions on these areas – but it can be invaluable in helping your wider understanding of financial markets if you have some awareness of what they are and their roles / purposes.

- **The money market**
    - Market for short term loan finance for businesses and households
    - Money is borrowed and lent for up to 12 months
    - Includes inter-bank lending i.e. the commercial banks providing liquidity for each other
    - Includes short term government borrowing e.g. 3-12 months Treasury Bills to help fund the government's budget (fiscal) deficit
- **Capital market**
    - Market for medium to longer term loan finance e.g. shares and bonds
    - Includes raising of finance by governments through the issue/sale of medium to long term government bonds for example 10 year and 20-year bonds (loans)
- **Foreign exchange market**
    - A market where currencies (foreign exchange) are traded. There is no single currency market – it is made up of thousands of trading floors
    - Gains or losses are made from exchange rates – speculative activity in the currency market is often high
    - The spot exchange rate is the price of a currency to be delivered now, rather than in the future
    - The forward exchange rate is a fixed price given for buying a currency today to be delivered in the future

Role of financial markets in the wider economy

A financial market is any exchange that facilitates the **trading of financial instruments**, such as stocks, bonds, foreign exchange, or futures/options contracts for primary commodities such as oil and gas.

What are the key roles of financial markets?

1. To facilitate saving by businesses and households: offering a secure place to store money and also earn interest
    - This allows households to smooth their consumption over time, and build up deposits/ funds for large purchases
2. To lend to businesses and individuals: financial markets provide an intermediary between savers and borrowers
    - Banks channel funds from savers to borrowers, who would otherwise be unable to connect in an efficient way
3. To allocate funds to productive uses: financial markets allocate capital to where the risk-adjusted rate of return is highest
4. To facilitate the final exchange of goods and services: they provide payments mechanisms e.g. contactless payments
    - Money is essential in a market economy in which division of labour is used
    - Money allows a much more efficient operation of an economy, because without money, there would be a barter system
5. To provide forward markets in currencies and commodities: forward markets allow agents to insure against price volatility

6. To provide a market for equities: allowing businesses to raise fresh equity to fund investment and growth
   - Businesses gain finance for investment and growth from a number of sources, including retained profits, loans from banks, borrowing from money and capital markets via issuing corporate bonds ("debt financing"), or gaining funds by issuing shares ("equity financing")

Characteristics of money
- Durable i.e. it needs to last
- Portable i.e. easy to carry around, convenient, easy to use
- Divisible i.e. it can be broken down into smaller denominations
- Hard to counterfeit - i.e. it can't easily be faked or copied
- Must be generally accepted by a population
- Valuable – generally holds value over time

Key functions of money
1. **Medium of exchange:** money allows goods and services to be traded without the need for a barter system. Barter systems rely on there being a double coincidence of wants between two people involved in an exchange
2. **Store of value:** this can refer to any asset whose "value" can be used now or used in the future i.e. its value can be retrieved at a later date. This means that people can save now to fund spending at a later date.
3. **Unit of account:** this refers to anything that allows the value of something to be expressed in an understandable way that allows the value of items to be compared.
4. **Standard of deferred payment**: this refers to the expressing of the value of a debt i.e. if people borrow today, then they can pay back their loan in the future in a way that is acceptable to the person who made the loan.

Distinction between narrow money and broad money
- **Narrow money**
  - The narrow money definition of the money supply is a measure of the value of coins and notes in circulation and other money equivalents that are easily convertible into cash such as short-term deposits in the banking system
- **Broad Money**
  - Broad money is a measure of the total money held by households and companies in the economy
  - Broad money is made up mainly of commercial bank deposits — which are essentially IOUs from commercial banks to households and companies — and currency — mostly IOUs from the central bank

Facilitating lending in the financial system
It is good to be aware of the different length of loans available from the financial system. The interest rate may depend on the length of the loan but also the credit-worthiness of the borrower including the risk of loan default.

Long-term loans	Medium-term loans	Short-term loans
Finances whole business over many years	Finances major projects or assets with a long-life	Finances day-to-day trading of a business
Examples:	**Examples:**	**Examples:**
Venture capital	Bank loans	Bank overdraft
Mortgages	Leasing	Trade creditors
Long-term bank loans	Hire purchase	Short-term bank loans
		Factoring

Debt finance

Debt financing means **borrowing money from an outside source** with the promise of paying back the borrowed amount, plus the agreed-upon interest, at a later date

| Bank loan | Bank overdraft |  Credit card | Mortgage |  Peer to peer lending | Corporate bond |

Key features of bank loans
1. Loan is provided over a fixed period (e.g. 5 years)
2. Rate of interest payable is either fixed or variable
3. Timing and amount of loans repayments are set by the lender e.g. a commercial bank
4. Non-performing loans ("bad debts") occur when the borrower is unable to repay some or all of the debt

Unsecured loans
- Money supported only by a borrower's creditworthiness, rather than by any type of collateral

Secured loans
- Money you borrow that is secured against an asset you own, usually your home

Equity finance

| Angel investors |  Venture capital | Stock market Listing | Crowd funding |

- Angel investors - individuals who inject capital for business start-ups
- Venture capital - firms specialising in building high risk equity portfolios
- Stock market listing - offering shares to public and institutional investors e.g. via an initial public offering (IPO)
- Crowd funding - raising capital from a large number of individual investors via platforms such as Crowd Cube

Banks

| Commercial banks | 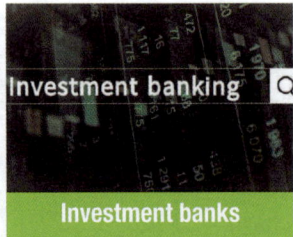 Investment banks | Internet banks | Shadow banks |

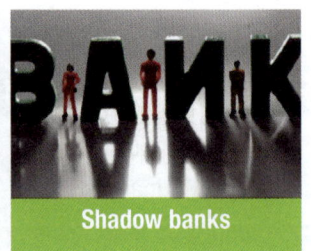

What are the main functions of a commercial bank?
- Commercial banks provide retail banking services to household and business customers
- Banks are **licensed deposit-takers** providing savings accounts
- They are **licensed to lend money** and thereby create money e.g. via bank loans, overdrafts and mortgages
- Commercial banks are nearly all profit-seeking businesses
- A bank's business model relies on charging a higher interest rate on loans than the rate paid on deposits
- This spread on their assets and liabilities is used to pay the operating expenses of a bank and make a profit

Banks **create credit** by extending loans to businesses and households. They do not always need to attract deposits from savers to do this. When a bank makes a loan, it credits their bank account with a bank deposit of the size of the loan/mortgage. At that moment, new money is created in the financial system.

How commercial banks make a profit
- Interest-rate spreads i.e. charging a higher interest rate on loans than the rate that is paid to savers
- Service fees - includes fees charged by a bank to borrowers when arranging loans
- Brokerage percentages - many banks provide currency and share-dealing services and charge a brokerage fee for doing so

How banks can fail
1. Run on the bank
    a. Depositors panic because of falling consumer confidence and withdraw their money fearing that the bank may collapse
    b. This creates a liquidity crisis for the bank, and they may need to find emergency sources of funding
    c. A bank may be unable to borrow money from other banks even on an overnight basis
2. High losses from bad debts / loan defaults as borrowers fail to repay
    a. Credit rating of bank declines and their share price falls – this makes it harder to raise fresh finance
    b. Banks are unable to pay the money it owes to others

Limits to credit creation by banks
- Market forces i.e. the scale of profitable lending opportunities
- Regulatory policies e.g. higher capital reserve requirements imposed by a central bank
- Behaviour of consumers and businesses e.g. decisions about how much of their debt to repay
- Monetary policy – the level of policy interest rates influences the demand for loans from households and businesses, for example the demand for business loans and mortgage loans in the housing market

Liquidity and credit risk for commercial banks

Liquidity risk
- Banks tend to attract short term deposits e.g. from savers
- They often lend for longer periods of time e.g. a 20-year mortgage
- As a result, a bank may not be able to repay all deposits if savers decide to withdraw their funds in one go
- To reduce their risk, commercial banks will try to attract long term deposits and also hold some liquid assets e.g. cash

Credit risk
- This is the risk to the bank of lending to borrowers who turn out to be unable to repay some or all of their loans.
- Credit risk can be controlled by research into the credit-worthiness of borrowers and also by banks having sufficient capital in reserve. Minimum capital reserves may be imposed by the financial authorities.

What are investment banks?
- An investment bank provides **specialised services** for companies and large investors:
    - Underwriting and advising on securities issues and other forms of capital raising
    - Advice on mergers, acquisitions and corporate restructuring
    - Trading on capital markets (bonds and equities)
    - Corporate research and private equity investments
- An investment bank trades and invests on its own account
- Commercial banks sometimes also provide investment banking services

4.4.2 MARKET FAILURE IN THE FINANCIAL SECTOR

> **What you need to know**
>
> Consideration of:
> - Asymmetric information
> - Externalities
> - Moral hazard
> - Speculation and market bubbles
> - Market rigging

Market failure occurs when a market fails to deliver an economically efficient and/or socially equitable allocation of scarce resources. Market failure is a justification for government intervention e.g. through financial regulation, although this too might lead to governmental / regulatory failures as a result. Before looking at specific examples of financial market failure, it is a good idea to refresh your understanding of the generic causes of market failure from Theme 1 microeconomics.

Asymmetric information
- This type of market failure exists when one individual or party has much more information than another individual or party and then uses that advantage to exploit the other party.
- Finance is a market in information – often a potential borrower (such as a small business) has better information on the likelihood that they will be able to repay a loan than the lender.

Externalities
- A negative externality exists when a market transaction has a negative consequence for a 3rd party
- A positive externality exists when a market transaction has a positive consequence for a 3rd party

Externalities in financial markets seem large – especially **contagion effects** – for example when there is a loss of trust and confidence between lenders and also between savers and financial institutions such as banks. A key concept is **systemic risk** – which means that, when one or more financial organisations experience problems, this can lead to the risk of a much wider damage to the economy and perhaps threaten the stability of much of the financial system. Millions of people can be affected negatively as a result.

> **Consider this excerpt from Bank of England research on the externalities from financial market instability:**
>
> "In finance, the private sector left to its own devices will never fully price the consequences of its actions. Although externalities exist in many markets and industries, those in finance seem especially large - contagion within the financial sector to other borrowers and lenders from interconnections and panics and fire sales, and the aggregate demand externality from the responses of heavily indebted households and businesses to shocks to income, interest rates or credit availability. Those externalities damage innocent third parties in the form of unemployment and lost income when the financial sector can't perform its normal intermediary functions and credit dries up."
>
> Source: www.bankofengland.co.uk/-/media/boe/files/speech/2017/regulation-for-financial-stability-the-essentials.pdf

The Bank of England estimates find that the **Global Financial Crisis** and recession that followed it left everyone in the UK around £20,000 worse off than had the crisis not materialised. In part this is the result of lower real income, output and employment across many sectors of the economy. It also comes from the fiscal costs of the bail-out of banks during the Global Financial Crisis and ensuing period of fiscal austerity.

Examples of 3rd parties who bear external costs (negative externalities) arising from financial crises:
1. Taxpayers (taxpayers bear the cost of bank bail-out costs and the impact of fiscal austerity)
2. Depositors (risk of lost savings if a bank collapses)
3. Creditors (a rise in unpaid debts can create difficulties)
4. Shareholders (lost equity from falling share prices)

5 Employees (lost jobs in finance and the wider economy especially if a financial crisis turns into a recession)
6 Government (increased fiscal deficit and national debt)
7 Businesses (reduced demand for goods and services and higher borrowing costs for those needing loans)

Moral hazard

Bail-outs may encourage riskier behaviour

Sub-prime loans were repackaged to investors

Moral hazard exists where an individual or organisation **takes more risks** because they know that they are covered by insurance, or they expect that the government will protect them (i.e. **bail them out**) from any damage incurred as a result of those risks.

Examples of moral hazard
- Individuals with large insurance policies to cover specific risks are more likely to claim against such policies
- Government bail-outs of commercial and investment banks encourage them to engage in riskier behaviour
- Sub-prime mortgage lenders prior to 2007 were able to repackage loans into bundles bought by other institutions

House price bubble | **Share price bubble** | **Bubble in crypto-currencies** | **Commodity price bubbles** | **Credit bubbles** | **Tulip Mania (1637)**

Speculation and market bubbles

What is a speculative bubble?
- A speculative bubble is a sharp and steep rise in asset prices such as shares, bonds, housing, commodities or crypto-currencies
- The bubble is usually fuelled by high levels of speculative demand which takes prices well above fundamental values

What factors can cause a speculative bubble?
- Behavioural factors e.g. the herd behaviour of investors
- Exaggerated expectations of future price rises (i.e. people expect property prices to carry on increasing)
- **Irrational exuberance** of investors – a term coined by Nobel-winning economist Robert Shiller
- A period of very low monetary policy interest rates – which encourages **risky investment** by people and by other agents in financial markets in search of higher yields

Market rigging
- This market failure is effectively collusion or abuse of the power resulting from operating in a concentrated market. Market rigging happens when some of the companies in a market act together to stop a market working as it should in order to gain an unfair advantage.
- When there is a small number of firms in a market, they may choose to work together to increase their joint profits and exploit consumers.
- The Competition and Markets Authority report on UK banking in August 2016 said that "the older and larger banks, which still account for the large majority of the retail banking market, do not have to work hard enough to win and retain customers and it is difficult for new and smaller providers to attract customers."
- Price rigging is illegal because it interferes with the natural market forces of supply and demand and harms consumers by inhibiting competition.

Monopoly power in financial markets

Market failure can arise when a market is not sufficiently competitive. The UK banking sector for example is dominated by a few very large banks, including the Lloyds Group, Barclays, the Royal Bank of Scotland (RBS), and HSBC. In term of market shares for all categories of business, the market is clearly oligopolistic. There are significant barriers to entry into the market which make life hard for new entrants as they seek to establish themselves and make a profit.

The total assests of UK banks from 2012-2023 in £ trillions

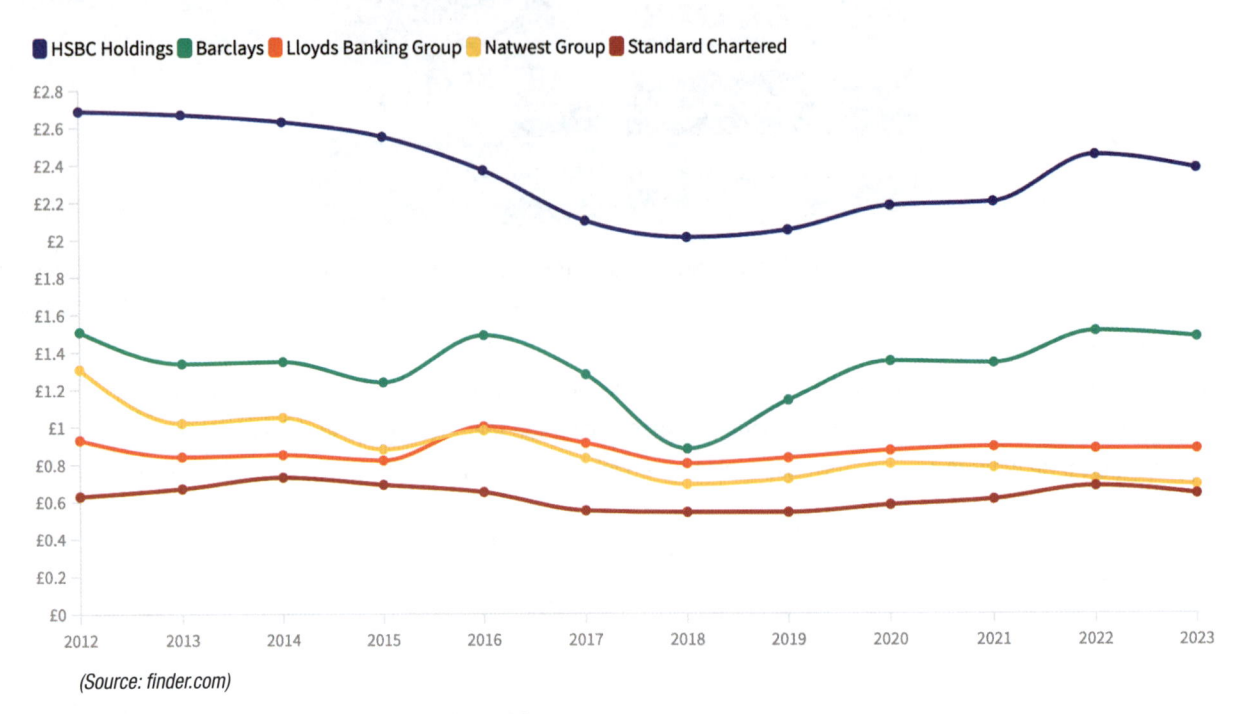

(Source: finder.com)

Examples of barriers to entry into commercial banking

1. Regulatory barriers – i.e. the need to be given a banking licence by the central bank
2. Natural or intrinsic barriers to entry – costs of entering the market including marketing costs, building IT and payments infrastructure
3. Strategic advantages of larger banks – including vertical integration, branch network, low rates of customer switching
4. First mover advantages including strong brand loyalty for established banks

Brand loyalty leads to low rates of consumer switching. This ties in with behavioural theories since the default choice of which bank to use is powerful in this market – leading to low rates of customer switching to other current accounts.

Primary banks in the UK 2023

Single pick: 'At which of these banks is the account held that you primarily use?'

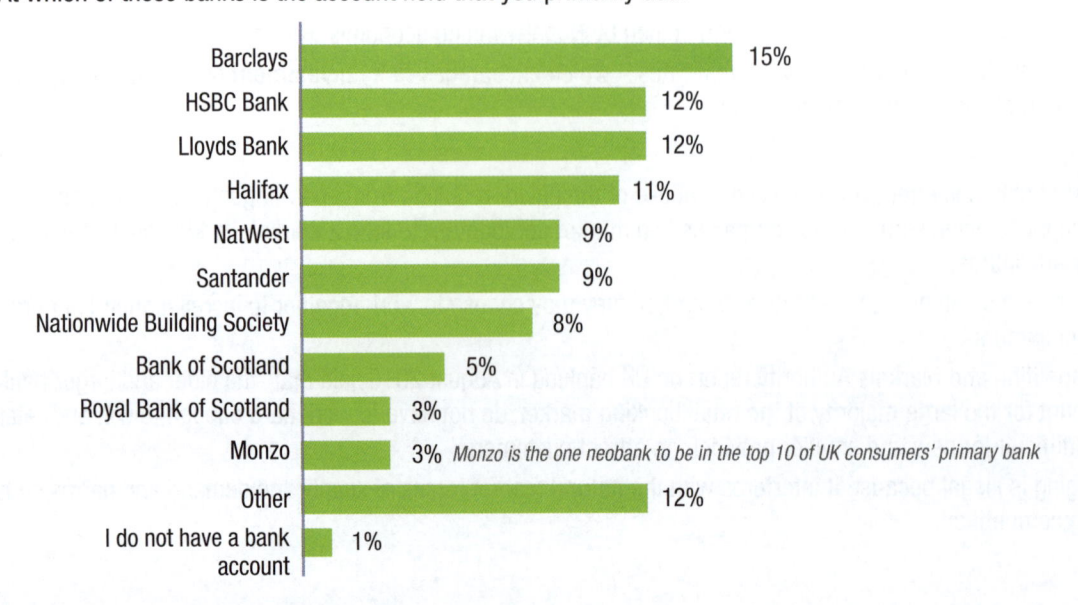

Bank	%
Barclays	15%
HSBC Bank	12%
Lloyds Bank	12%
Halifax	11%
NatWest	9%
Santander	9%
Nationwide Building Society	8%
Bank of Scotland	5%
Royal Bank of Scotland	3%
Monzo	3%
Other	12%
I do not have a bank account	1%

Monzo is the one neobank to be in the top 10 of UK consumers' primary bank

However, although the commercial banking industry in the UK remains an oligopoly, there are signs that it is becoming more contestable. The competitive threat from challenger banks, FinTech and new market entrants is increasing. Competitive threats are emerging from examples such as these:

- Established challengers: First Direct, Metro Bank, TSB, Virgin Money
- Online banks: Atom, Monzo, Zopa, Tandem
- Supermarket banks: Asda Money, M&S Bank, Sainsbury's Bank
- FinTech companies offering banking services: Azimo, iZettle, Curve
- The Next Wave - digital platform companies such as Google and Apple

Systemic risk in financial markets

What is systemic risk?

- Systemic risk is the possibility that an event at the micro level of an individual bank / insurance company could then trigger instability or collapse of an industry or economy
- The Global Financial Crisis (GFC) illustrated how deeply **inter-connected** the financial world has become
- Shocks in one location (e.g. the USA) or one asset class (e.g. sub-prime mortgages) can have a sizable impact on the stability of institutions and markets around the world
- Since the crisis, financial regulators have tried to make the banking system less vulnerable to economic shocks and **create firewalls** to prevent damage from systemic risk

Professor Joseph Stiglitz on the Financial Sector

"*I have likened the financial sector to the brain of the economy: it is central to the management of risk and the allocation of capital. It runs the economy's payment mechanism. It intermediates between savers and investors, providing capital to new and growing businesses. When it does its functions well, economies prosper, when it does its jobs poorly, economies and societies suffer.*"

4.4.3 ROLE OF CENTRAL BANKS

What you need to know

Key functions of central banks:
- Implementation of monetary policy
- Banker to the banks – lender of last resort
- Banker to the government
- Role in regulation of the banking industry

COMMON ERROR ALERT!
You must not assume that all central banks operate in the same way as the Bank of England – they are not all fully independent of government; they do not all operate inflation targets etc.

Examples of central banks
- Bank of England (UK)
- European Central Bank (ECB) for member nations of the Euro Area
- United States Federal Reserve
- Bank of Japan
- Bank of Canada
- Reserve Bank of Australia
- Reserve Bank of New Zealand

Main functions of a central bank
- Monetary policy function
    - Setting of the main monetary policy interest rate
    - Quantitative easing (QE)
    - Exchange rate intervention (managed/fixed currency systems)
- Financial stability and regulatory function
    - Supervision of the wider financial system
    - Prudential policies designed to maintain financial stability
- Policy operation functions
    - Lender of last resort to the banking system
    - Managing liquidity in the commercial banking system
    - Overseeing the payments systems used by banks / retailers / credit card companies
- Debt management
    - Handling the issue and redemption of government debt (bonds)

Implementation of monetary policy
- Monetary policy involves changes in interest rates, the supply of money and credit and exchange rates to influence the economy
- Monetary policy is broader than simply changes in interest rates and it is important to be aware that there is no such thing as "the" interest rate as there are thousands of different types of interest rate on savings and loans at any one time!
- The impact of changes in interest rates was covered in Theme 2 macro so please refresh your understanding of how movements in interest rates can affect different macroeconomic variables

Monetary policy in the UK
- The Bank of England has been independent of the UK government since 1997
- The main aim of the Bank of England is to promote monetary and financial stability
- Monetary stability means stable prices and confidence in the currency. Stable prices are defined by the Government's inflation target, which the Bank seeks to meet through the decisions taken by the Monetary Policy Committee (MPC)
- The policy interest rate (Bank Rate) is set by the Monetary Policy Committee. The 2% inflation target is set by the UK government.

The Monetary Policy Committee (MPC)
- The Monetary Policy Committee does a thorough assessment of the UK economy 8 times a year
- They look at a range of demand/supply-side indicators
- The interest rate decision is taken after this
- Key issue is the strength of inflationary pressures and the inflation forecast for the UK over the next two years
- Inevitably there is a lot of uncertainty
- Monetary policy affects both the demand and the supply-side of the economy, it does not operate in isolation

Expansionary Monetary Policy	Deflationary Monetary Policy
Reducing nominal and real interest rates	Higher interest rates on both loans and savings
Steps to expand the supply of credit from the banking system e.g. via QE	Tightening of credit supply (i.e. loans from banks become harder to get)
Devaluation of the external value of the exchange rate	Revaluation of the external value of the exchange rate

Expansionary monetary policy

This is a monetary stimulus and involves changes in monetary policy designed to increase aggregate demand including lower policy interest rates and measures to increase the supply of credit.

Contractionary monetary policy

Deflationary policies designed to lower the level / growth of aggregate demand to help control inflationary pressure. This can involve a rise in interest rates, tighter controls on bank lending and perhaps attempts to cause an exchange rate appreciation which would lower import prices.

Evaluating a decade of very low interest rates

Central banks around the world cut interest rates sharply during the 2007-2009 financial crisis. Interest rates then remained at historic lows for many subsequent years close to or below 0% in most developed economies.

Case for maintaining very low interest rates

1. Inflationary pressures in many advanced countries have remained weak giving little justification for raising interest rates to control inflationary pressures
2. Some economists argue that the Phillips Curve has flattened, i.e. the trade-off between unemployment and inflation has weakened, this implies that an economy can operate at a higher level of aggregate demand and employment without risking an acceleration of inflation
3. Maintaining low interest rates help to stimulate capital investment which increases a country's long-run productive potential
4. Low interest rates as part of an expansionary monetary policy have been helpful in supporting aggregate demand and output during an era of fiscal austerity in many developed countries
5. Keeping interest rates low may have helped to reduce the risks of price deflation and also contributed to maintaining a competitive currency which has helped export industries

Counter-arguments

In evaluation, a number of economists argue that advanced economies such as the UK would now benefit from a period of (perhaps gently) rising interest rates. Here are some of the arguments in support of this view:

1. A rise in monetary policy interest rates would help to control demand for credit, softens the growth of the money supply and therefore help to control demand-pull inflation especially when unemployment is very low
2. Increased mortgage rates may cause a slowdown in house price inflation and therefore help to make property more affordable over time especially for hard-pressed young families who struggle to rent
3. Higher interest rates will increase the return to saving – raising effective disposable incomes for retirees
4. Higher interest rates reduce the risk of mal-investment by business that only goes ahead because of the cheap cost of capital
5. Interest rates need to rise moderately now so that central banks can cut them in the event of a negative external shock. They need to give themselves some policy leeway when the economy next experiences a recession

Risks from raising interest rates

- High levels of unsecured debt – there is a risk of a significant slowdown in consumption if retail credit becomes more expensive to service e.g. expensive credit cards
- Higher interest rates might choke off much needed business investment e.g. in new house-building and renewable energy capacity
- Rise in interest rates might cause the sterling exchange rate to appreciate thus making exports less competitive, leading to an export slowdown and a worsening external deficit
- Higher interest rates make government debt more expensive
- Higher interest rates might lead to an economic slowdown which could hit share prices, pension fund assets and dividend incomes

Quantitative easing (QE)

What is quantitative easing?
- One of the main aims of quantitative easing is to increase the supply of money available for banks to lend.
- It is an alternative strategy to that of cutting interest rates.
- The Bank of England's MPC's quantitative easing (QE) programme, where the Bank creates new money to buy financial assets totalled £895 billion of assets in July 2021 - £875 billion of which were government bonds and £20 billion of commercial debt. More recently the Bank of England has been reducing the stock of bonds it holds. This is called Quantitative Tightening (QT).

How does QE operate?
- QE involves the introduction of new money into the national supply by a central bank.
- In the UK the Bank of England creates new money (electronically) to buy assets (mainly government bonds) from insurance companies, pension funds and commercial banks.
- Increased demand for government bonds causes an increase in the market price of bonds.
- A higher bond price causes a fall in the yield on a bond (this is because there is an inverse relationship between bond prices and yields).
- Those who have sold their bonds may use the extra funds/cash to buy assets with higher yields such as shares of listed businesses and corporate bonds.
- Commercial banks receive cash, and this increases their liquidity. This may encourage them to lend out more money.

Summary of the main channels through which quantitative easing is supposed to work:
1. **Wealth effect** - lower yields (interest rates) lead to higher share and bond prices
2. **Borrowing cost effect** - QE lowers the interest rate on long term debt such as government bonds and mortgages
3. **Lending effect** - QE increases the liquidity of banks and increased lending from banks lifts incomes and spending in the economy
4. **Currency effect** - lower interest rates has the side effect of causing the exchange rate to weaken (a depreciation) which helps exports

> **Exam Tip** Quantitative easing is a complex topic. Here are two key takeaway points:
> 1/ Buying government bonds raises their price and, in doing so, drives down the yield, or interest rate, they offer.
> 2/ Replacing government bonds with cash in the economy increases liquidity.

Arguments in favour of quantitative easing
- Gives a central bank an extra tool of monetary policy besides changing interest rates
- Increasing the size of the monetary base helps to lower the threat of price deflation. Without QE, the fall in real GDP would have been deeper and the rise in unemployment greater
- Lower long-term interest rates have kept business confidence higher and given the commercial banking system extra deposits to use for lending
- QE can lead to a depreciation of the exchange rate which helps to improve the price competitiveness of export industries

According to the UK Bank of England
"Monetary easing (including lower interest rates and QE) led to lower unemployment and higher wages than would have otherwise been the case, which particularly benefited younger age groups because they are more likely to work than older groups and because their job prospects tend to be more pro-cyclical."

Source: www.bankofengland.co.uk/-/media/boe/files/working-paper/2018/the-distributional-impact-of-monetary-policy-easing-in-the-uk-between-2008-and-2014.pdf

Criticisms of quantitative easing (with specific reference to the UK economy)

1. Ultra-low interest rates can distort the allocation of capital and also keep alive zombie companies (note: this is a key criticism of Hayekian/Austrian school).
2. QE contributed to a surge in share prices and property values, the latter has worsened housing affordability for millions of people and also contributed to an increase in rents which worsened the geographical immobility of labour.
3. QE did little to cause an increase in bank lending to businesses, many commercial banks have become more risk averse and charge higher interest rates to business customers.
4. QE contributed to a decade of ultra-low interest rates which was bad news for millions of people who rely on interest from their savings.
5. Low interest rates and bond yields are a worry for pension fund investors because they worsen their deficits. If companies must pay more into their employee pension schemes, they therefore have less money to spend on investment which could harm productivity growth in the long run.

Regulation of the financial system

How are we to safeguard the financial system to ensure that another crisis does not arise in the future? Regulation of financial markets attempts to overcome one or more **market failures**. Since the Global Financial Crisis, there has been a significant increase in financial regulation although a number of commentators argue that there have been insufficient structural reforms of the industry and that risks remain of another financial crisis in the years ahead.

Who are the main regulators of the UK financial system?

- Financial Policy Committee (FPC)
- Prudential Regulation Authority (PRA)
- Financial Conduct Authority (FCA)
- Competition and Markets Authority (CMA)

What are the main aims of financial market regulation?

1. Protect against the consequences of market failure
   a. Protect the interest of consumers
   b. Limit the monopoly power of commercial banks by encouraging increased competition
   c. Protect borrowers from excessively high interest rates on loans e.g. on unsecured credit
   d. Improved access to affordable finance services – this is key for growth and development and prevention of poverty in many countries
   e. Balance the interests of uninformed consumers with sophisticated sellers of financial services (i.e. address problems arising from information asymmetry)
2. Encourage confidence in the economy and government
   a. Promote capital investment and sustainable long run growth
   b. Support trust in the banking system so that people and businesses are willing to save
3. Allow the central bank (e.g. the Bank of England) to perform its other roles such as lender of last resort
   a. Prevent/mitigate systemic risk within financial markets that might damage the economy

Financial Policy Committee of the Bank of England – "macro prudential regulation"

- The FPC's main role is to identify, monitor, and take actions to remove or reduce risks that threaten the resilience of the UK financial system as a whole
- The FPC publishes a **Financial Stability Report** identifying key threats to the stability of the UK financial system
- The FPC has the power to instruct commercial banks to change their capital buffers
- When the FPC decide that the risks to the financial system are growing, they may tell the commercial banks and other lenders to increase their capital buffers to help absorb unexpected losses on their assets (bad debts etc.)
- These capital buffers are part of "macro-prudential policy" - prudent means being careful at times of uncertainty.

UK Prudential Regulation Authority (PRA) – "micro prudential regulation"

- The PRA is also part of the Bank of England and is responsible for the prudential regulation and supervision of around 1,700 banks, building societies, credit unions, insurers and major investment firms
- The PRA has a particular focus on the solvency of individual firms within specific financial markets such as:
  - Insurance providers
  - Buy-to-let mortgage lenders
  - Credit unions
  - Other specialist lenders

Examples of regulation in financial markets

Liquidity ratios
- A liquidity ratio is the ratio of liquid assets held by a bank on their balance sheet to their overall assets
- Commercial banks need to hold enough liquidity to cover expected demands from their depositors
- In the wake of the Global Financial Crisis the Basel Agreement requires commercial banks to keep enough liquid assets, such as cash and bonds, to get through a 30-day market crisis
- A liquidity ratio may refer to a reserve assets ratio for a bank which sets the minimum liquid reserves that a bank must maintain in the event of a sudden increase in withdrawals
- Liquid Asset Ratio = (cash & balances with central banks + government bonds) divided by a bank's total assets

Capital ratios
- A commercial bank's capital ratio measures the funds it has in reserve against the riskier assets it holds that could be vulnerable in the event of a crisis.
- Banks must maintain sufficient capital which includes money raised from selling new shares to investors and also their retained earnings (i.e. non-distributed profits)

Counter-cyclical capital buffers for banks
Commercial banks are required to hold capital in the form of buffers which can be used to absorb losses during an economic downturn, enabling them to continue lending to the economy. Without these buffers, banks are more likely to cut back lending in the face of losses, making any downturn worse. The counter cyclical capital buffer rate for the UK banking system is currently set at 2%. The FPC can raise this when financial risks are rising and relax it when financial risks are easing. Counter-cyclical buffers can be summarised as following:

- **Upswing in credit cycle** – banks required to build up extra capital reserves
- **Downswing in credit cycle** – banks have more capital to help absorb losses

Macro and micro prudential policies
Since the global financial crisis, regulators have placed increased emphasis on prudential regulation i.e. putting in place safeguards for the stability of the financial system

- **Micro-prudential** involves stronger regulation of individual financial firms such as commercial banks, payday lenders and insurance companies. It also seeks to protect individual depositors / borrowers.
- **Macro-prudential** regulation seeks to safeguard the financial system as a whole i.e. protect against systemic risk. Macro-prudential regulation seeks to make the system more resilient.

Extension idea: regulation through leverage ratios

- The leverage ratio is an indicator of the ability of a bank or building society to absorb losses
- Leverage ratio = capital / exposures
- The leverage ratio refers to the share of the total value of a firm's assets and its other commitments (referred to as 'exposures') that is funded with capital capable of absorbing losses while a firm is a 'going concern'.
- The lower the leverage ratio, the more that a bank or building society relies on debt to fund their activities
- In 2015, the FPC directed the Prudential Regulation Authority (PRA) to require each major UK commercial bank and building society to meet a leverage ratio requirement and hold buffers over that requirement
- The FPC have introduced a mortgage loan to income (LTI) cap which limits the number of mortgages extended at LTI ratios of 4.5 or higher to 15% of a lender's new mortgage lending. The proportion of high loan-to-income mortgages that banks and building societies can underwrite is restricted to 15% of new mortgages

Stress tests for commercial banks

Stress tests assess commercial banks' ability not just to withstand severe shocks, but also to maintain the supply of credit to the real economy under severe pressure. Stress tests use **tail-end risk events** i.e. economic outcomes that lie well outside the mainstream forecasts. A failure to adequately insure against tail-end risk was a major reason behind the severity of the global financial crisis a decade ago.

The 2018 UK financial markets stress scenario was more severe than the global financial crisis. In the stress test, UK GDP fell by 4.7%, the UK unemployment rate rose to 9.5%, UK residential property prices fell by 33% and UK commercial real estate prices fell by 40%. The scenario also included a sudden loss of overseas investor appetite for UK assets, a 27% fall in the sterling exchange rate index and Bank Rate rising to 4%. (Source: FPC Report, July 2019)

> *"The financial system is dynamic and adaptive. So, any financial regulatory regime will need to be adaptive if it is to contain risk within this system."*
> **Andy Haldane, BoE, November 2017**

Key summary of financial market failures and examples of interventions in the UK

Financial market failure	Current examples of interventions (including regulations) designed to address the causes and consequences of market failure
Externalities arising from financial instability	Depositor protection for families with savings Increased capital requirements for commercial banks Stress tests for commercial banks and other financial businesses Limits to highly-leveraged mortgage lending (LTV ratios)
Herd behaviour and speculative bubbles in financial markets	Financial Policy Committee created to oversee financial stability Monetary Policy Committee can raise interest rates to reduce the risk of an unsustainable housing / asset price boom Possible regulation of use of volatile crypto-currencies
Market rigging / monopoly power of the banks	Tougher competition policy for anti-competitive behaviour Price cap on interest rates charged by pay-day lending companies More licences to challenger banks to improve contestability
Asymmetric information and complexity of financial products	Penalties / compensation for mis-selling of PPI Improved financial literacy education in schools and colleges Auto-enrolment in workplace pensions (mandated choice)

4.5.1 PUBLIC EXPENDITURE

What you need to know

Distinction between capital expenditure, current expenditure and transfer payments

Reasons for the changing size and composition of public expenditure in a global context

Significance of differing levels of public expenditure as a proportion of GDP on:
- Productivity and growth
- Crowding out
- Level of taxation
- Living standards
- Equality

> **COMMON ERROR ALERT!**
> You should remember that current and capital spending by the government will have different effects on the economy – current spending is likely to affect AD alone whereas capital spending is likely to affect both AD and LRAS.

Current and capital spending

Government spending is split into categories based on whether the money is spent on an asset that lasts a number of years (such as a new building or vehicle) or is spent on things that are used up (like salaries of civil servants or teachers). The former is referred to as "capital" spending, and the latter as either "resource" or "current" spending.

> **COMMON ERROR ALERT!**
> Do not confuse current spending with transfer payments. A transfer payment is a payment made by the government for which there is no exchange of goods/services e.g. welfare spending.

Examples of current spending

- Salaries of NHS employees
- Drugs used in health care 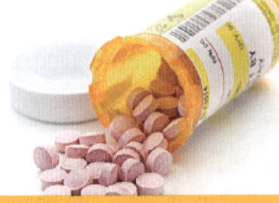
- Road maintenance budget 
- Army logistics supplies 

Examples of capital spending

- Construction of new motorways and bridges
- New equipment in the NHS 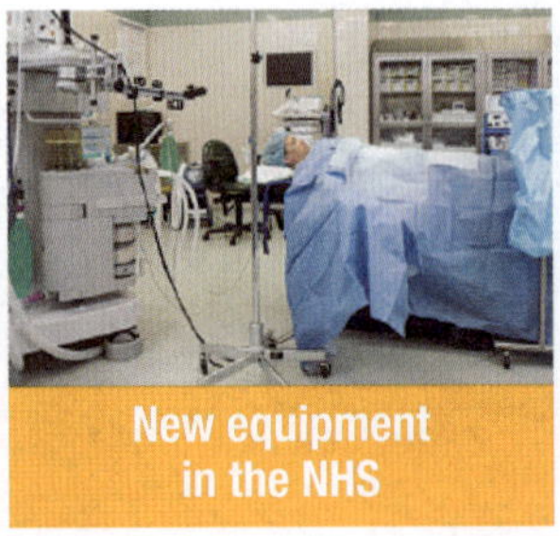
- Flood defence schemes 
- Extra defence equipment 

Significance of government spending

- A key component of aggregate demand
- Can have a regional economic impact e.g. from spending on regional infrastructure projects
- Important in providing public goods and goods with positive externalities
- Can help to achieve greater equity in society

How government spending can affect household incomes:
- Welfare state transfers
  - Universal child benefits / unemployment benefit
  - Public (state) pensions
  - Targeted welfare payments - linked to income
- State-provided services (which offer "in-kind benefits" to people)
  - Education – helps to reduce inequality of market incomes
  - Health care – state provided health services
  - Social housing e.g. provided by local authorities
  - Employment training

What are the justifications for government spending?
1. To provide a socially efficient level of public goods and goods with positive externalities and overcome market failures
   a. Public goods and goods with positive externalities tend to be under-provided by the private sector
   b. Improved and affordable access to education, health, housing and other public services can help to improve human capital, raise productivity and generate gains for society as a whole
2. To provide a safety-net system of welfare benefits to supplement the incomes of the poorest in society – this is also part of the process of redistributing income and wealth. Government spending has an important role to play in controlling / reducing the level of relative poverty
3. To provide necessary infrastructure via capital spending on transport, education and health facilities – an important component of a country's long run aggregate supply
4. Government spending can be used to manage the level and growth of AD to meet macroeconomic policy objectives such as low inflation and higher levels of employment
5. Government spending can be justified as a way of promoting equity.
6. Well-targeted and high value for money public spending is also a catalyst for improving economic efficiency and competitiveness e.g. from infrastructure projects

The free market agenda on the size of government
- **Free market economists** are sceptical of the impact of government spending in improving the supply-side
- They argue that **lower taxation and tight control of government spending and borrowing** is required to allow the private sector of the economy to flourish (this is associated with the crowding-out theory)
- They believe in a **smaller sized state sector** so that in the long run, the overall burden of taxation can come down and thus allow the private sector of the economy to grow and flourish

The gap between total government spending and tax revenue shows the annual budget deficit if G>T or surplus if G<T

Crowding out theory

What is crowding-out?
The crowding out view is that a rapid growth of government spending leads to a transfer of scarce productive resources from the private sector to the public sector where productivity might be lower. It can also lead to higher taxes and interest rates which then squeezes profits, investment and employment in the private sector.

Increased government borrowing may lead to higher demand for loanable funds and therefore a rise in market interest rates e.g. on bonds. This might then increase borrowing costs for private sector businesses.

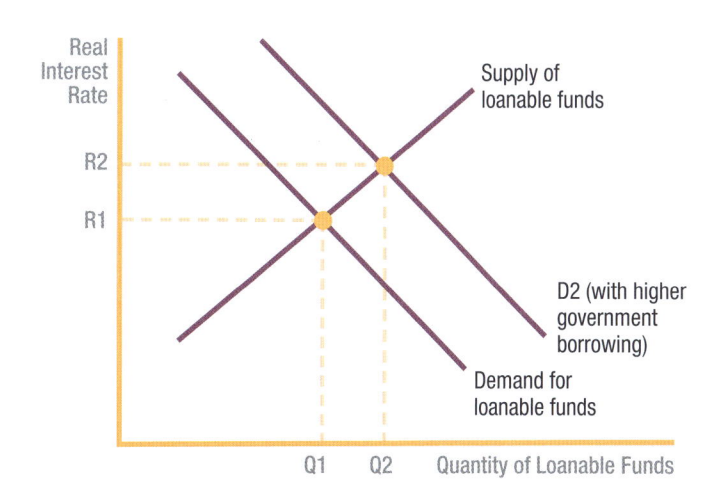

Evaluating the crowding out theory

1. The probability of 100% crowding-out is remote, especially if an economy is operating below its capacity and if there is a plentiful supply of saving available to purchase newly issued state debt
2. Keynesian economists are opposed to fiscal austerity and argue instead that fiscal deficits **crowd-in** private sector demand and investment
3. Well-targeted, timely and temporary increases in government spending can absorb under-utilised capacity and provide a strong positive multiplier effect that eventually generates extra tax revenue
4. Another criticism of the basic crowding-out theory is that the available supply of loanable funds is not limited to domestic sources, external finance is available from other countries

What is crowding-in?

When an increase in government spending/investment leads to an expansion of economic activity (real GDP) which in turn incentivises private sector firms to raise their own levels of capital investment and employment. Crowding-in is a view supported by Keynesian economists.

Fiscal austerity – macro and micro effects of cuts in government spending

Micro impacts

- Output, jobs and profits in construction, transport & defence sectors
- Effective demand for goods and services e.g. welfare caps might change the pattern of demand for goods and services
- Cuts in pension spending might lead some people to delay their retirement

Macro impacts

- Multiplier effects of cuts in public sector spending and employment
- Lower fiscal deficit might help investor confidence / attract investment
- Risks of deflationary pressures if cutting spending creates excess capacity (negative output gap)
- Bank of England more likely to keep interest rates at very low levels
- Effects on real income and relative poverty of households

4.5.2 TAXATION

What you need to know

Distinction between progressive, proportional and regressive taxes

Economic effects of changes in direct and indirect tax rates on other variables:
- Incentives to work, tax revenues: the Laffer curve
- Real output and employment, the price level (e.g. CPI)
- Income distribution
- The trade balance (X-M) and FDI flows

Direct and indirect taxes

Direct taxes

- Direct taxation is levied on income, wealth and profit
- Direct taxes include income tax, inheritance tax, national insurance contributions, capital gains tax, and corporation tax (a tax on business profits)
- The burden of a direct tax cannot be passed on to someone else

Indirect taxes

- Indirect taxes are usually taxes on spending
- Examples of indirect taxes include excise duties on fuel, cigarettes and alcohol and Value Added Tax (VAT) on many different goods and services together with the sugar tax
- Producers may be able to pass on an indirect tax – depending on price elasticity of demand and supply

> **COMMON ERROR ALERT!**
> Students often write incorrectly about progressive and regressive taxes. In both cases it is likely that the amount of revenue generated from each type of tax by high earners will be higher. It is vital that you consider the proportion of income spent in each category of tax!

Progressive taxes

What are progressive taxes?
- With a progressive tax, the **marginal rate of tax** (MRT) rises as income rises.
- As people earn more, the rate of tax on each extra pound goes up. This increases the average rate of tax.

Income tax in the UK is a progressive tax:
- Income tax on earned income is charged at three rates: the basic rate, the higher rate and the additional rate.
- For 2024-25 these rates are 20%, 40% and 45% respectively.
  - Personal tax allowance (zero tax) up to £12,570
  - Basic rate taxed on taxable income between £12,571 and £50,270
  - Higher tax taxed on taxable income between £50,271 and £125,140
  - Additional 45% marginal tax rate on any taxable income in excess of £125,140

(Income tax rates are slightly different in Scotland)

The burden of income tax on households in different quintiles is shown in the table below:

Percentage of gross income taken by different taxes in the UK						
	Lowest 20% of Income	2nd Quintile	3rd Quintile	4th Quintile	Highest 20% of Income	All households
Income Tax	2.5	4.4	8.2	11.2	16.9	11.8

Regressive taxes

What are regressive taxes?
- With a regressive tax, the rate of tax paid falls as incomes rise – i.e. the average rate of tax is lower for people on higher incomes. Examples include: duties on tobacco and alcohol.
- A tax is said to be regressive when low income earners pay a higher proportion or percentage of their income in tax than high income earners.

Consider data shown in the table which indicates that VAT is regressive as are indirect taxes when taken together.

Percentage of Gross Income taken by different taxes in the UK						
	Lowest 20% of Income	2nd Quintile	3rd Quintile	4th Quintile	Highest 20% of Income	All people
VAT	11.0	7.9	7.7	7.0	5.5	6.8
Duty on alcohol	1.5	1.0	1.0	0.9	0.7	0.9
Duty on tobacco	2.8	1.7	1.3	0.6	0.3	0.8
All indirect taxes	28.1	19.1	17.8	15.3	11.3	15.3

The Laffer curve

What is the Laffer curve?
- It is a (supposed) relationship between economic activity and the rate of taxation which suggests there is an optimum tax rate which maximises total tax revenue
- Why might total tax revenues fall if the tax rate increases?
    - Increased rates of tax avoidance – greater incentive to seek out tax relief, make maximum use of tax allowances
    - Greater incentive to evade taxes (illegal) – i.e. non–declaration of income and wealth
    - Possible disincentive effects in the labour market – depending on which taxes have been increased
    - Possible "brain drain" effects – including the loss of highly skilled and high-income taxpayers

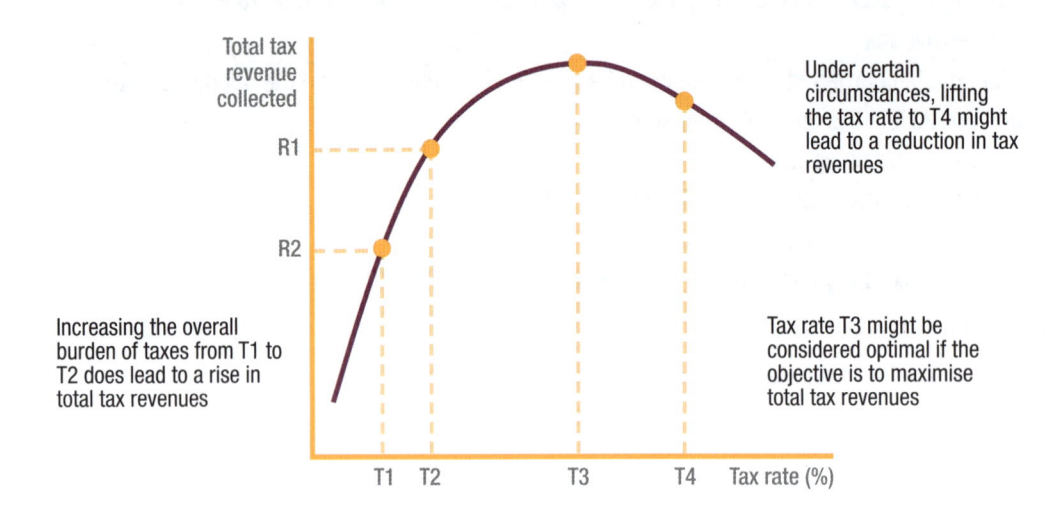

[Laffer curve diagram: Total tax revenue collected on y-axis, Tax rate (%) on x-axis. Curve rises from T1 to peak at T3, then falls. R1 corresponds to T2, R2 corresponds to T1. Annotations: "Increasing the overall burden of taxes from T1 to T2 does lead to a rise in total tax revenues"; "Under certain circumstances, lifting the tax rate to T4 might lead to a reduction in tax revenues"; "Tax rate T3 might be considered optimal if the objective is to maximise total tax revenues"]

Evaluation of the Laffer Curve concept
1. Lower top rate taxes might increase income inequality
2. Little evidence that high top rates of income tax is a barrier to inward migration of skilled labour
3. Many people are on fixed hours / zero hour contracts – so tax rates may have little bearing on work incentives
4. For some people, tax cuts will cause them to take more leisure time instead of work especially at higher wages/ earnings
5. There is a Keynesian explanation for some aspects of the Laffer Curve – cuts in direct and indirect taxes increase real disposable income and therefore lead to higher consumer spending and aggregate demand

Taxation and aggregate demand
- Changes in tax rates and tax allowances have direct and indirect effects on the level/growth of AD
- Changes in income tax and national insurance have a direct effect on people's disposable incomes
- Changes in corporation tax affect the post-tax profit available for businesses to invest
- Changes in employers' national insurance affect the cost of employing extra workers in the labour market
- A change in value added tax brings about changes in retail prices and affects the real incomes of consumers

Taxation and aggregate supply
- Changes in tax rates and tax allowances have a direct and indirect effect on SRAS and LRAS
- Changes in VAT affect business costs e.g. the VAT applied when buying component parts / supplies
- Changes in direct taxes can influence work incentives
- Changes in business taxes might affect the level of foreign direct investment into a country
- Taxes can also affect the incentive to start a business or to spend money on research and development

Chain of reasoning and evaluation – impact of cuts in corporation tax

Government cuts the rate of corporation tax	→	Businesses get to keep a larger percentage of their operating profits	→	Increase in post-tax profitability may lead to a rise in planned investment
Creates a positive multiplier effect on demand, output and employment	←	Increased capital spending is an injection into the circular flow model	←	Investment can be by both domestic and overseas businesses

Evaluation
- Impact depends on the scale of the tax cut and whether it is long-lasting or considered to be a temporary measure
- Many factors affect capital investment e.g. the pace of technological change and strength of market competition
- Some extra investment may lead to a loss of jobs through capital-labour substitution effects

Analysis of the possible impact of a rise in the standard rate of VAT

Macroeconomic objective	Comment on the effect of a rise in VAT
Inflation	Higher in short run as businesses pass on tax
Economic growth	Slower as real incomes and demand fall
Unemployment	Higher if aggregate demand weakens
Balance of trade in goods & services	Improved – falling incomes may cause demand for imports to contract
Spare capacity in the economy	Rising spare capacity from weaker demand
Business investment	Decline if businesses are hit by lower profits and weaker consumer spending
Government fiscal (budget) balance	Short run improvement from higher taxes but risk of falling revenues in medium term

4.5.3 PUBLIC SECTOR FINANCES

What you need to know
- Distinction between automatic stabilisers and discretionary fiscal policy
- Distinction between a fiscal deficit and the national debt
- Distinction between structural and cyclical deficits
- Factors influencing the size of fiscal deficits
- Factors influencing the size of national debts
- The significance of the size of fiscal deficits and national debts

Fiscal policy is an important instrument for a government wanting to manage the level of and rate of growth of aggregate demand in order perhaps to reduce cyclical fluctuations in output and employment.

Automatic stabilisers and discretionary fiscal policy
- **Discretionary fiscal changes** are deliberate changes in direct and indirect taxation and government spending – for example, extra capital spending on roads or more resources into the NHS
- **Automatic stabilisers** are changes in tax revenues and government spending that come about automatically as an economy moves through the business cycle

Explanations for automatic stabilise:

1. **Tax revenues:** when the economy is expanding rapidly the amount of tax revenue increases which takes money out of the circular flow of income and spending
2. **Welfare spending:** a growing economy means that the government does not have to spend as much on means-tested welfare benefits such as income support and unemployment benefits
3. **Budget balance and the circular flow:** a fast-growing economy tends to lead to a net outflow of money from the circular flow. Conversely during a slowdown or a recession, the government normally ends up running a larger budget deficit. During a recession, revenue is likely to be lower due to less income earned, less profits made and fewer goods being bought and at the same time government expenditure on transfer payments e.g. income support and unemployment benefit

Government borrowing and bond interest rates

When a government borrows it issues debt in the form of **bonds**. The **yield on a bond** is the interest rate paid on state borrowing. Purchasers of British government bonds for example include pension funds, insurance companies and overseas investors. The percentage yield on sovereign (government) debt has been low in recent years for countries such as the UK and Germany but higher for nations such as Greece which has had several emergency bail-outs in recent times.

Distinction between fiscal deficit and the national debt

What is government borrowing?

Public sector borrowing is the amount the government must borrow each year to finance their spending in excess of taxation.

What is national debt?

Public sector debt is a measure of the accumulated national debt owed by the government sector.

Public sector debt

Public sector debt is owed by central and local government and also by state-owned corporations.

A government runs a fiscal (budget) deficit when total government spending exceeds revenues over the course of a year.

Distinction between structural and cyclical deficits

The size of the fiscal deficit is influenced by the current state of the economy:

- During an economic boom, when real GDP is expanding, and the economy is operating above its potential (i.e. there is a positive output gap), then tax receipts are relatively high and spending on unemployment benefit is low. This reduces the level of government borrowing
- The reverse happens in a recession when borrowing tends to be high. This is because a recession leads to rising unemployment and falling real incomes which leads to an increase in state spending on welfare assistance

The structural fiscal deficit is that part of the deficit that is not related to the state of the economy. This part of the deficit will not disappear when the economy recovers from a recession. It thus gives a better guide to the underlying level of the deficit than the headline figure. The structural deficit cannot be directly measured so it has to be estimated.

Factors influencing the size of fiscal deficits

- **Cyclical factors**
    - Rate of unemployment – higher unemployment reduces tax revenues and increases welfare spending
    - Consumer spending – strong consumer spending increases VAT revenue
    - Business profits – rising business profits increases revenue from corporation tax
    - Automatic stabilisers – in an economic downturn, the fiscal deficit rises as G increases and T falls
- **Long run factors**
    - Size of the welfare state – e.g. the scale and breadth of welfare assistance available
    - Relative level of welfare benefits e.g. compared to incomes
    - Demographic factors e.g. ageing population, the impact of net inward migration of labour
    - Size of the tax base and tax rates – i.e. is an economy moving towards a lower or higher tax burden
    - Efficiency of the public sector - e.g. the productivity of workers in the NHS and education in delivering services

Factors influencing the size of national debts

Scale of government spending
- Current spending on public services
- Investment spending e.g. on infrastructure
- Spending on providing social welfare

Level of tax revenues
- Size of the tax base e.g. how many in work and their incomes
- Efficiency of tax collection, scale of tax avoidance & evasion

Cost of servicing debt and state bail-outs
- Yield on new and existing government bonds
- Willingness of lenders to give the government new credit
- Government rescue of businesses can add to public sector debt

Significance of the size of fiscal deficits and national debts

Is a high level of government debt dangerous?

"A high level of government borrowing will result in money having to be spent repaying that debt. This can lead to both a reduction in investment and a requirement on future generations to continue paying off these debts, which could in turn have a negative impact on national well-being." (Source: ONS)

Public debt is the total stock of debt issued by a government yet to be re-paid – it is also known as the National Debt.

Arguments that rising national debt creates economic problems:
1. High fiscal deficits cause rising debt interest payments.
2. This interest burden has an opportunity cost for less interest on debt could free up extra spending on health and education. In 2024/2025, gross debt interest payments for the UK are forecast to be £73.5bn.
3. An increase in the national debt is likely to cause higher taxes in the future. This will cut the disposable incomes of tax payers and reduce growth in the private sector.
4. It might be unfair if the rising tax burden falls more heavily on future generations of tax payers rather than people who benefit from government spending now.

Counter arguments – the case for government borrowing:

Since 1970, the UK has run a budget surplus in only six years – it is normal for the government to borrow money.

1. A rise in borrowing to fund extra government spending can have powerful effects on AD, output and employment when an economy is operating below full capacity output.
2. There is an automatic rise in the budget deficit to cushion the fall in AD caused by an external economic shock. A higher fiscal deficit is needed to lift AD back towards pre-recession levels and support an economic recovery.
3. If a fiscal stimulus works, then the budget deficit will improve as a result of higher tax revenues and reductions in welfare spending. A growing economy helps to shrink debt as a percentage of GDP.
4. It makes sense for a government to borrow money if interest rates are low and if the deficit is being used for investment to improve a nation's infrastructure to aid competitiveness. Borrowing to invest can bring about much needed improvements in public services such as education, health, transport and social housing. It can lead to an increase in long run aggregate supply and therefore support long-run economic growth.

Bond yields, fiscal deficit and financing the national debt

Government bonds are fixed interest securities. This means that a government bond pays a fixed annual interest – this is known as the coupon. The coupon (paid in £s, $s, Euros etc.) is fixed but the yield on a bond will vary.

The yield is effectively the interest rate on a bond and the yield will vary inversely with the market price of a bond.
- When bond prices are rising, the yield will fall
- When bond prices are falling, the yield will rise

Here is an example:
- When a 10-year bond has a market price of £5,000 and pays a fixed annual interest (coupon) of £200
- Then the yield = (£200 / £5,000) x 100% = 4%
- Consider what happens when the market price of the bond falls e.g. because of speculative selling of bonds by investors
- Assume the bond price falls to £4,300
- The interest (coupon) on the bond remains fixed at £200
- Therefore, the yield on the bond = (£200 / £4,300) x 100% = 4.65%
- There is an inverse relationship between the market price of a bond and the yield on a bond
- When bond prices fall, then the yield on the bond increases

The yield on UK government bonds has been declining over the last 18-20 years. Indeed, despite a high level of national debt and continuing budget deficits, the nominal yield on 10-year bonds was below 2 per cent from 2016 to mid 2022. In mid 2024, it was around 4%, which is still historically low. In this sense, the UK government can borrow cheaply if it wants to increase investment spending. There is a strong overseas and domestic demand for government bonds and yields have also fallen due to the programme of quantitative easing by the Bank of England. QE involves the BoE buying government debt which leads to the market price of debt rising and the yield on bonds falling.

Bond yields have also dropped in many other countries including Germany, Spain and Japan. The drop in ten-year bond yields for Greece is perhaps a reflection of an improved macroeconomic situation for a country that has suffered badly from the financial crisis, very high unemployment and price deflation.

Exam Tip Essay questions on fiscal policy are common, perhaps asking students to evaluate the extent to which running a fiscal/budget deficit is a problem for an economy, or whether high government debt is a problem, or whether government debt / fiscal deficits should be reduced. These are worth practising, especially under timed conditions.

4.5.4 MACROECONOMIC POLICIES IN A GLOBAL CONTEXT

What you need to know

Use of fiscal policy, monetary policy, exchange rate policy, supply-side policies and direct controls in different countries, with specific reference to the impact of:
- Measures to reduce fiscal deficits and national debts
- Changes in interest rates and the supply of money
- Measures to reduce poverty and inequality
- Measures to increase international competitiveness

Use and impact of macroeconomic policies to respond to external shocks to the global economy

Measures to control global companies' (transnationals') operations:
- Regulation of transfer pricing
- Limits to government ability to control global companies

Problems facing policymakers when applying policies:
- Inaccurate information
- Risks and uncertainties
- Inability to control external shocks

Fiscal austerity

Fiscal austerity is the term used to describe policies designed to reduce the size of a government fiscal deficit and eventually control / lower the size of the outstanding national debt. In the UK, austerity policies were in place from 2010 in the aftermath of the Global Financial Crisis. Austerity has also been imposed in countries such as Greece and Italy as part of the bail-outs of national governments by the European Union and the International Monetary Fund.

To what extent is fiscal austerity helpful or, in contrast, damaging to a country's economic performance?

Overview of policies to reduce a fiscal deficit
This can be achieved in a number of ways:
Cuts in government spending
- Controlling public sector pay including wage freezes or limiting annual pay awards to 1%
- Limiting welfare entitlement
- Privatisation of state assets so that a government no longer has to cover losses
- Reductions in the size and scale of government subsidies

Higher taxes
- Higher indirect taxes such as VAT rising to 20%
- Cutting tax allowances or ending certain tax reliefs
- Bringing in new taxes e.g. new environmental taxes or taxes on digital businesses

Supply-side policies to encourage growth
- This approach focuses on the argument that a growing and a more competitive economy will be a more effective way of cutting the deficit and the debt in the long-term.
- Stronger GDP growth increases tax revenues because the tax base widens, and people/businesses are earning higher incomes and profits.
- In a progressive tax system, expanding incomes and perhaps higher prices will lead to a faster growth of tax receip.
- Growth cuts a deficit as a % of GDP because the denominator (GDP) has increased.

Arguments in favour of fiscal austerity
1. Reducing the budget deficit and the national debt is in the long run interests of economy – for example it helps to keep UK taxes lower and can avoid the problem of the state sector crowding-out investment and growth in the private sector.
2. Shrinking state encourages private sector growth in the long-run.
3. There is a high opportunity cost of the amount spent each year on debt interest.
4. Cutting the fiscal deficit can improve investor confidence and might attract more FDI into the UK.
5. The upturn of the economic cycle is time for government to borrow less – ahead of another downturn or recession – it makes sense to be running stronger budget finances before the economy enters a cyclical slowdown or downturn.

Arguments against fiscal austerity
1. Austerity is self-defeating especially if it leads to price deflation and lower employment, because this depresses employment and investment which are vital to sustain tax revenues in the future.
2. Government bond yields are relatively low – so this is an opportune time to invest more because infrastructure investment will increase both AD and LRAS.
3. Wrong to cut state spending when economy is in a liquidity trap (i.e. unresponsive to low interest rates).
4. Economic growth is needed to pay back the debt and fiscal austerity makes this harder to achieve.
5. There are damaging social consequences from fiscal austerity – it risks increasing inequalities of income and can be a factor in more families having to use food banks and borrowing at very high interest rates from payday lenders.
6. Pay freezes in the public sector under the previous Conservative government have harmed recruitment and led to growing shortages of key workers in education and healthcare. This leads to longer waiting times and threatens the delivery of important merit goods.

The Keynesian view

Keynesian economists tend to favour the active use of fiscal policy as the main way of managing demand and economic activity. They argue that the fiscal multiplier effects of increased government spending can be high, and that fiscal policy is a powerful device for helping to stabilise confidence, demand, output and jobs especially after severe external economic shocks.

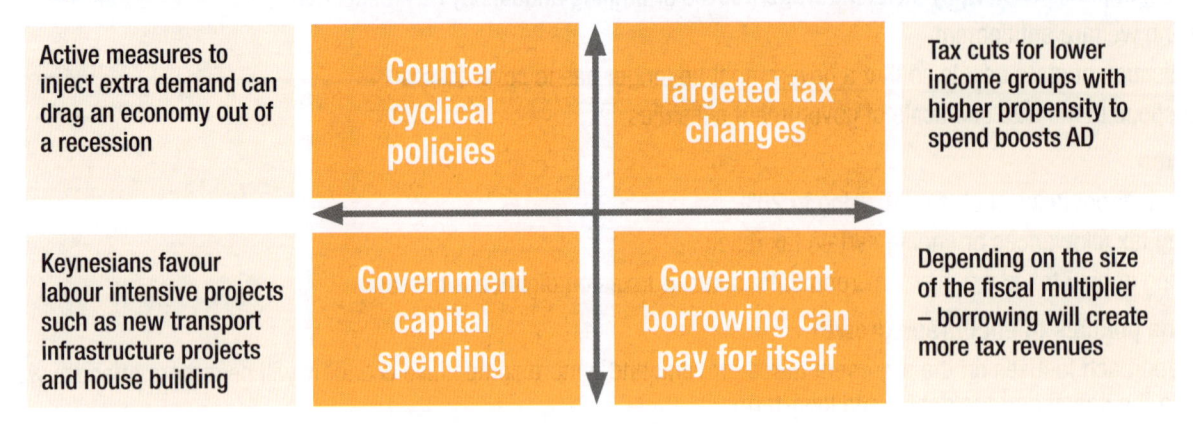

Active measures to inject extra demand can drag an economy out of a recession	**Counter cyclical policies**	**Targeted tax changes**	Tax cuts for lower income groups with higher propensity to spend boosts AD
Keynesians favour labour intensive projects such as new transport infrastructure projects and house building	**Government capital spending**	**Government borrowing can pay for itself**	Depending on the size of the fiscal multiplier – borrowing will create more tax revenues

Policies to reduce poverty and inequality

It is widely believed that persistent and deep relative poverty is a major barrier to growth and development. Hence the importance attached by many countries to introducing effective poverty-reduction strategies. These policies will vary from country to country and it is important to consider where a nation is in their economic development when assessing what is possible and also the likely impact.

According to a report on poverty in the UK published by the Joseph Rowntree Foundation in 2017, *"Poverty wastes people's potential, depriving our society and economy of the skills and talents of those who have valuable contributions to make. An estimated £78bn of public spending is linked to dealing with poverty and its consequences. This includes spending on healthcare, education, justice, child and adult social services."* Poverty and inequality are multi-dimensional and have huge consequences for economic well-being and the scale and depth of mental health issues in the UK.

Examples of policies designed to reduce inequality of income and wealth

Welfare systems
- Direct cash transfers to poorer households – conditional cash transfers link cash benefits to households dependent on certain actions e.g. having their children immunised or attending school regularly
- Measures to introduce a basic pensions system – which in theory would allow households to save more of their disposable income or increase spending on necessities such as education or better health care
- Government subsidies for transport and child care to increase labour market participation

Labour market policies
- Employment protection including legal protections for workers wanting to be represented by a trade union
- Minimum wage laws - offering a guaranteed pay floor for lower-paid workers
- Trials to introduce a universal basic income
- Incentives to improve business training / productivity which ultimately will increase productivity. Productivity is the biggest single driver of improved wages over time

Tax reforms
- Progressive taxes on the income / wealth of the rich
- Taxing profits of businesses to fund state spending including measures to curb tax avoidance by transnational **corporations**

In many countries, the problem of working poverty has become more acute particularly in the decade or more since the Global Financial Crisis. In the UK, people in work are increasingly likely to be in relative poverty (i.e. not earning enough to take household income above 60 per cent of median income). This has been linked to the rapid rise of the gig economy and the increasing monopsony power of major employers.

Globally, the percentage of people living in working poverty – defined broadly as earning less than $3.65 a day (PPP adjusted) varies widely by region as shown in the table below. Nearly two-thirds of people in work in sub Saharan Africa earn below this threshold.

Population living on less than PPP$3.65 a day	% of population
Regions	
Arab States	12.6
Asia and the Pacific	3.6
Caribbean	6.4
Europe and Central Asia	0.6
Latin America	3.31
South Asia	7.9
Sub-Saharan Africa	32.8
Least developed countries	39.1
World	6.93

(Source: Our World in Data)

Policies to increase international competitiveness

This is an extremely broad topic covered in more detail in section 4.1.9

Overview of policies to improve competitiveness

- **Improving the functioning of labour markets**
  - Investment in all levels of education and training including early years education and technical/vocational courses for school and college leavers
  - Encouraging inward migration of skilled workers – some nations have chosen a points-based system of immigration targeting skilled occupations where there are labour shortages
  - Improvements in management quality
- **Critical (core) infrastructure investment**
  - Better motorways, ports, hi-speed rail, new sewers – infrastructure gaps can severely hamper businesses
  - Investment in clean energy networks to help support sustainable growth
  - Communications e.g. super-fast broadband, 4G and 5G networks
- **Supporting enterprise / entrepreneurship**
  - Improved access to business finance e.g. for start-ups and small & medium-sized enterprises
  - Incentives for business innovation and invention including lower taxation on profits from patented products
  - Reductions in business red tape
- **Macroeconomic stability**
  - Maintaining low inflation / price stability to help confidence
  - A sustainable and more competitive banking system to improve the flow of finance for investment
  - A competitive exchange rate versus major trading partners – for some countries this has involved moving towards managed floating exchange rates and/or a competitive devaluation of a fixed exchange rate

Broadly, policies to increase competitiveness can be divided between those which favour a free-market approach – focusing for example on lower taxes, less regulation and trade liberalisation, and those that make the case for selected government intervention in markets designed to address the market failures that can worsen competitiveness.

World Competitiveness Rankings for 2024

Country	Ranking	Country	Ranking	Country	Ranking
Singapore	1	Norway	10	United Kingdom	28
Switzerland	2	US	12	Kazakhstan	35
Denmark	3	China	14	Japan	38
Ireland	4	Korea	20	India	39
Hong Kong	5	Germany	24	Botswana	55

Policies to respond to external shocks in the global economy

What are external shocks?

Shocks are unexpected changes in the economy that can affect variables such as inflation and the growth rate of GDP. In an inter-connected global economy, events in one part of the world can quickly affect many other countries. For example, the Global Financial Crisis (GFC) brought about recession in many countries and financial distress in many regions. It also led to a fall in FDI flows into poorer countries and increased pressure on governments in rich nations to cut overseas aid budgets.

One distinction to make is between **demand and supply-side** shocks. Analysis of both encourages you to use the AD-AS analysis (including the diagrams!) you will have developed as part of Theme 2 in Year 12 economics.

Demand-side shocks

- Economic downturn / recession in a major trading partner
- Unexpected tax increases or cuts to government spending programmes
- Financial crisis causing bank lending /credit to fall and which spreads to more than one country/region
- Unexpected changes in monetary policy interest rates
- Significant job losses announced in a major industry

Supply-side shocks

- Steep rise/fall in oil and gas prices or other commodities traded in the world economy
- Political turmoil / strikes
- Natural disasters causing a sharp fall in production and damage to infrastructure
- Unexpected breakthroughs in production technologies which can lead to unexpected gains in productivity
- Significant changes in levels of labour migration into/out of a country

> **Exam Tip** A change in oil prices will have a complicated effect on the economies of different countries. Try to understand a little about the economic context facing each country. For example, is a country a net importer or an exporter of oil and gas? What scope do policy-makers have to change variables such as interest rates and taxation in response to an external shock?

Shocks can be positive (i.e. helpful in driving economic growth) and negative (e.g. a deep financial crisis which reduces confidence, spending and investment).

When analysing the impact(s) of an external shock, always remember to go back to the main macroeconomic objectives. Consider the likely impact on:

- Real GDP growth
- Inflation (demand-pull and cost-push)
- Unemployment
- Competitiveness
- The trade balance
- Government finances
- Possible impact on inequality

Policies to absorb the effects of an economic shock

Not every country has the ability to respond quickly and effectively to external shocks. Much depends on how severely they are affected by economic events.

1. Floating exchange rates (i.e. is there scope for a depreciation?)
2. Freedom to set / adjust monetary policy when conditions change - does the central bank have autonomy to change interest rates or bring in unconventional policies such as QE?
3. Geographically and occupationally mobile / flexible labour force - a more flexible labour force helps an economy adjust to shocks that change the pattern of exports
4. Strong non-price competitiveness of domestic businesses - this helps make demand and output more resilient to fluctuations in the global economy
5. A diversified economy that is not over reliant on a few sectors
6. Strong fiscal position (stabilisation funds) e.g. strong finances give a government the scope to run a fiscal stimulus when aggregate demand falls

Keynesian approach to external economic shocks

- Keynesians believe that free markets are volatile and not self-correcting in the event of an external shock
- The free-market system is prone to lengthy periods of recession & depression
- Economies can remain stuck in an "underemployment" equilibrium
- In a world of stagnation or depression, direct state intervention may be essential to restore confidence and lift demand
- Keynes was one of the first economists to criticise the economics profession for adhering to unrealistic assumptions

Measures to combat the power of transnational corporations (TNCs)

Multinationals or transnationals are large businesses that operate in a number of countries. They often separate their production between various locations or have their different divisions – Head Office and Administration, Research and Development, Production, Assembly, Sales – separated around a continent or the globe.

Transnational corporations (TNCs) have become increasingly significant in the global economy. Indeed, research produced in 2016 by the World Bank found that nearly 70 of the world's top 100 'economies' are corporations with Walmart, Apple and Shell richer than Russia, Belgium and Sweden. TNCs have the effect of 'grouping' nations together systematically through both their production and supply chains and via the different markets they serve with products. For example, the UK and Malaysia are linked together by the TNC Dyson. The famous bagless vacuum cleaners are designed and sold in the UK but manufactured in Malaysia.

What is the scale of tax avoidance?

In recent years, much of the attention has been on issues such as tax avoidance strategies of corporations from advanced nations. US firms booked more profits in Ireland than in China, Japan, Germany, France and Mexico combined according to a 2018 paper on tax havens and multinational activity published by Professor Gabriel Zucman. The standard corporate tax rate on profits in Ireland is 12.5% but, considering tax reliefs and allowances, the effective corporate tax rate in Ireland is estimated to be just 5.6%. The OECD estimates that around $480bn is lost each year due to tax avoidance and much of this revenue would have accrued to governments in developing and emerging countries. Multinationals avoid nearly £6 billion a year in the UK according to Treasury estimates. In 2018, the FT reported that multinationals were paying significantly lower tax rates than before the 2008 global financial crisis.

A major trend in the last decade is that many countries have lowered their main corporation tax rates (some see this as a "**race to the bottom**") to help them attract foreign direct investment whilst at the same time, taxation on personal income has risen. This is a key reason why opposition to TNC activities in the global economy has cemented.

Reforms to reduce corporate tax avoidance

1. Some governments want to introduce a standard minimum tax rate on corporate profits across all of the advanced countries
2. Others favour introducing new digital services taxes specifically for businesses such as Amazon, Apple, Facebook and Google

What is transfer pricing?

Transfer pricing is also known as **profit shifting** and it happens when a TNC moves the profits they have made from subsidiaries in a high tax country to other subsidiaries in a lower tax nation. Usually this happens when a TNC sets up an **internal trade** - for example a **royalty** for using a trademark or a charge for using component parts which then affects the costs of each subsidy and helps to ensure that lower profits are booked in the higher-tax economy.

Potential benefits of TNCs for host countries

The potential benefits of TNCs on host countries include:

1. Provision of significant employment and training to the labour force in the host country
2. Transfer of skills and expertise, helping to develop the quality of the host labour force
3. TNCs add to the host country GDP through their spending, for example with local suppliers and through capital investment
4. Competition from MNCs acts as an incentive to domestic firms in the host country to improve their competitiveness, perhaps by raising quality and/or efficiency
5. TNCs extend consumer and business choice in the host country
6. Profitable MNCs are a source of significant tax revenues for the host economy (for example on profits earned as well as payroll and sales-related taxes)

Potential drawbacks of TNCs on host countries

The potential drawbacks of TNCs on host countries include:

1. Domestic businesses may not be able to compete with MNCs and some will fail
2. TNCs may not feel that they need to meet the host country expectations for acting ethically and/or in a socially-responsible way
3. TNCs may be accused of imposing their culture on the host country, perhaps at the expense of the richness of local culture
4. Profits earned by TNCs may be remitted back to the TNC's base country or low tax haven rather than reinvested in the host economy
5. TNCs may make use of transfer pricing and other tax avoidance measures to significantly reduce the profits on which they pay tax to the government in the host country

EXAM SUPPORT THEME 4 REVISION CHECKLIST

Globalisation

Characteristics of globalisation

Factors contributing to globalisation in the last 50 years

Impacts of globalisation and global companies on individual countries, governments, producers and consumers, workers and the environment

Specialisation and trade including absolute and comparative advantage

Patterns of trade (both geographical and commodity pattern of trade)

Trading blocs and the World Trade Organization (WTO)

Terms of trade

Free Trade Areas

Customs Unions

Single Markets (including the EU)

Monetary Unions (including Euro Zone)

Restrictions on free trade including import tariffs, quotas and other non-tariff barriers

Impact of protectionist policies on consumers, producers, governments, living standards, equality

Balance of payments

Components of the balance of payments: current account, capital account, financial account

Causes of deficits and surpluses on the current account

Measures to reduce a country's imbalance on the current account

Significance of global trade imbalances

Exchange rates

Floating exchange rates

Fixed exchange rates

Managed exchange rates

Factors influencing floating exchange rates

Competitive devaluation/depreciation of the currency and its consequences

International competitiveness

Measures of international competitiveness: including relative unit labour costs

Factors influencing international competitiveness

Policies to improve competitiveness

Poverty and Inequality

Distinction between absolute poverty and relative poverty

Measures of absolute poverty and relative poverty

Causes of changes in absolute poverty and relative poverty

Distinction between wealth and income inequality

Measurements of income inequality

Causes of income and wealth inequality within countries and between countries

Impact of economic change and development on inequality

Significance of capitalism for inequality

Emerging and developing countries

Measures of development (HDI & others)

Factors influencing growth and development

Strategies influencing growth and development

Trade liberalisation

Foreign direct investment

Privatisation

Human capital investment

Microfinance

Buffer stock schemes

Infrastructure investment

Overseas aid

Debt relief

Role of World Bank

Role of International Monetary Fund

The financial sector

Roles of financial markets (bond, currency, equity and money markets)

Causes of financial instability

Market failure in the financial sector

Speculative bubbles

Herd behaviour

Externalities from financial market failure

Market rigging in financial markets

Role of central banks in financial markets

Policies to support financial stability

Role of the state in the macroeconomy

Public (government) expenditure

Crowding out theory

Taxation - direct and indirect taxes

Distinction between progressive, proportional and regressive taxes

Economic effects of changes in direct and indirect tax rates on other variables:

Distinction between automatic stabilisers and discretionary fiscal policy

Distinction between a fiscal deficit and the national debt

Distinction between structural and cyclical fiscal deficits

Factors influencing size of fiscal deficits

Factors influencing size of national debts

The significance of size of fiscal deficits and national debts

Macroeconomic policies in a global context

Use and impact of policies to respond to external shocks to the global economy

Use and impact of policies to reduce inequality

Measures to control global companies' (transnationals') operation

NOTES